Thomas McGuane

Twayne's United States Authors Series

Frank Day, Editor

Clemson University

TUSAS 586

Thomas McGuane
Photograph by Dexter Westrum.

Thomas McGuane

Dexter Westrum

Ottawa University

Twayne Publishers
A Division of G. K. Hall & Co. • Boston

Thomas McGuane
Dexter Westrum

Copyright 1991 by G. K. Hall & Co.
Published by Twayne Publishers
A division of G. K. Hall & Co.
70 Lincoln Street
Boston, Massachusetts 02111

Copyediting supervised by Barbara Sutton.
Book production by Janet Z. Reynolds.
Book design by Barbara Anderson.
Typeset by Graphic Sciences Corporation, Cedar Rapids, Iowa.

10 9 8 7 6 5 4 3 2 1

The paper used in this publication meets the minimum requirements
of American National Standard for Information Sciences—Permanence
of Paper for Printed Library Materials, ANSI Z39.48–1984. ∞™

Printed and bound in the United States of America.

Library of Congress Cataloging-in-Publication Data

Westrum, Dexter.
     Thomas McGuane / Dexter Westrum.
          p.   cm. — (Twayne's United States authors series ; TUSAS 586)
     Includes bibliographical references and index.
     ISBN 0-8057-7631-1
     1. McGuane, Thomas—Criticism and interpretation.   I. Title.
II. Series.
PS3563.A3114Z94   1991
813'.54—dc20   91-12442

For Jane, Brenda, Eileen, and Debra

Contents

Preface

My goal in this study is to introduce readers to the essential ideas in the work of Thomas McGuane, a prime example of a contemporary American serious writer—one who steadfastly maintains his own vision of life and writes with a secure knowledge of the American canon. Indeed, Thomas McGuane has been on the verge of membership in that canon for several years. His work follows a direct line from the great writers of our past, his romantic protagonists continually embodying the American frontier and transcendental traditions as they confront the often-frustrating realities of modern-day existence in quest of life's infinite possibilities. Since McGuane is a writer who seeks to "report to us from the real world," I have sought to discuss his work in terms of what he has to tell us about the adventure of life in our time. Here I have been particularly drawn to his depiction of the relationships between parents and protagonists, his sense of the residue of crassness in American society, his characterizations of women, and how these elements influence his protagonists as they search for fulfillment.

Originally, I wanted to investigate the relationship between the serious writer and the publishing industry. What I found was not exactly what I expected. I had imagined a sort of market-casing intrigue among the author, his agents, and his editors and a sort of create-a-market wheeler-dealerism on the part of the publishing companies. What I discovered was that although serious literature is not exactly an endangered species, its continued existence is nothing dedicated readers should take for granted. To begin with, the serious writers are for the most part left to their own decisions about what they are going to write. Editors help them do what they want to do, and agents attempt to market—though rarely for security-creating sums—what they have written. Not much intrigue there. I also discovered that in light of corporate takeovers, publishing is more and more falling victim to a bottom-line mentality and that serious readers are not thought to be a significant market. In a country of 240 million people, a hardcover sale of serious fiction at 20,000 copies is a significant event. Were it not for the efforts of publishers like Seymour Lawrence, renowned as a tireless champion of serious literature, and Gary Fisketjon, who originated the Vintage Contemporary series while a fledgling editor at Random House, and of independent booksellers, persons impassioned about maintaining serious fiction, the tradition of American literature would be in danger of disintegrating to popcorn–genre novels and romans à clef of the rich and randy.[1] I exaggerate, perhaps, but my point is this: the serious writer and reader owe a large debt to a small group of people.

As I progressed through the work, I tried to capture a sense of the development of McGuane the writer. Accordingly, the chapters in this volume begin with (a) an overview of what McGuane was attempting to accomplish as he created each book and (b) a brief plot summary. These are followed by highlights from significant reviews, in an effort to chart the establishment of McGuane's reputation within the literary community, and by my own analysis of each work.

I have not sought to analyze McGuane's work directly through the details of his life. During our two mornings of interviewing in the summer of 1988, I found McGuane to be a consummate practitioner of the art of good talk. I have thus often let him speak for himself in the biographical sections of this book as I laid out what appear to be the central and motivating forces behind his life and work. Where necessary I have drawn on his remarks to others to construct the biographical portrait. Since McGuane is an often-interviewed writer, I saw no need to burden him with questions he had already discussed thoroughly. If direct parallels exist between the life and the work, perceptive readers can find them easily enough.

Neither have I asked the author to interpret his own work. While I have checked and double-checked the biographical portions of this study with Thomas McGuane, I have maintained the position that the task of criticism was mine. I therefore assume credit for any useful insights unearthed, as well as for any misreadings, misinterpretations, or flights of fancy of which I may be guilty.

I gratefully acknowledge permission from Salem Press, Inc., to reprint portions of this material that appeared in different form in "Thomas McGuane" in *Critical Survey of Long Fiction: Supplement,* © 1987 by Frank N. Magill.

I have accrued many debts in the completion of this project; let me acknowledge some of them here. First and last, I thank Jane Westrum, who in more than 20 years of marriage has always been my first and most demanding reader, for understanding the necessity of reading and writing in my life. I also thank especially my student assistant Shawna Bethell Paramore for her extensive library searches and the staff of Myers Library at Ottawa University for securing promptly through interlibrary loans the articles and reviews she discovered. I thank as well Professors Robert Solotaroff, Arthur Geffen, Kent Bales, Chester Anderson, Robert

Silberman, and Marty Roth of the University of Minnesota for encouraging my interest in Thomas McGuane when it took shape in that most inchoate of forms, the dissertation chapter; colleagues in the Western American Literature Association and the American Culture Association who listened and responded to earlier versions of these ideas as they appeared in papers; Professor Cynthia Taylor of the University of Southern Colorado, Professors Patrick Moore and Michael Kleine of the University of Arkansas at Little Rock, and Nancy Cook of the State University of New York at Buffalo for sustained and useful conversations about McGuane's work; and Dean Peter Sandstrom and Professor Lora K. Reiter of Ottawa University for continuing moral support.

In addition, I thank Liz Traynor Fowler and Barbara Sutton of Twayne Publishers and Professor Frank Day of Clemson University for their work as editors; Seymour Lawrence, Gary Fisketjon, Candida Donadio, and John Hawkins for insights into American publishing; Richard Locke, Michael Palmer, William Hjortsberg, Bud Shrake, and Jim Harrison for telephone conversations; Karen Trott, Peter Herdrich, David Blythe, Julie and Harmony King, Jim and Brenda Margadant, and Mel Spinar for food, shelter, and friendship during a summer of interviews; Dennis Dorgan for accompanying me to Montana; Laurie and Anne McGuane for their hospitality; and Thomas McGuane, a warm and gracious man, for providing me with more time and encouragement than I had a right to expect.

Finally, I thank my own version of the Three Graces, former students Brenda Rees, Eileen Scallen, and Debra Williams, whose lives and careers continue to affirm and encourage the teacher in me; I ask these three to share with Jane in the dedication of this book.

Chronology

1939   Thomas McGuane born on 11 December in Wyandotte, Michigan.

1960   Studies fiction writing with Gerald Chapman at Harvard University summer school.

1962   B.A., Michigan State University.

1965   M.F.A., Yale University.

1966   Lives in Spain and Italy.

1967–1968   Studies under Wallace Stegner Fellowship at Stanford University.

1969   Publishes *The Sporting Club.*

1971   Publishes *The Bushwhacked Piano.* Receives Richard and Hinda Rosenthal Award from the American Academy. Movie version of *The Sporting Club* (screenplay by Lorenzo Semple, Jr.) released.

1973   Publishes *Ninety-two in the Shade.* Nominated for National Book Award.

1974   Writes and directs movie version of *Ninety-two in the Shade.*

1975   *Rancho DeLuxe* (original screenplay) and *92 in the Shade* (film) released.

1976   *Missouri Breaks* (original screenplay) released and published.

1977   Wins team roping championship at Gardiner Rodeo.

1978   Publishes *Panama.*

1980   Publishes *An Outside Chance: Essays on Sport. Tom Horn* (original screenplay with Bud Shrake) released.

1981   Publishes *Nobody's Angel.* Takes a more aggressive role in the management of his late father's manufacturing company.

1984   Publishes *Something to Be Desired.* Gary Fisketjon includes *The Bushwhacked Piano* in the first wave of Vintage Contemporaries.

1985   Signs contract with Seymour Lawrence.

1986   Publishes *To Skin a Cat*. Wins cutting horse championship
        at Houston Stock Show.

1987   Sells his late father's manufacturing company.

1989   Receives Montana Centennial Award for Literature. *Cold
        Feet* (original screenplay with Jim Harrison) released. Wins
        Montana cutting horse championship for fourth time. Pub-
        lishes *Keep the Change*.

Chapter One
The Shaping of a
Person of Letters

Thomas McGuane is respected by reviewers and critics and is seen as an author of note by the serious reading public. He has published seven noteworthy novels, a book of personal essays, and a collection of short fiction. Early in his career McGuane was heralded as one of the most promising writers of his generation, one with a good chance of achieving election to the canon of American literature. He appeared on the front page of the *New York Times Book Review* and was compared favorably with Ernest Hemingway, William Faulkner, and Saul Bellow. *The Bushwhacked Piano,* his second published novel, won the Rosenthal Award, given annually for the best novel that sells the least, and *Ninety-two in the Shade,* his third, was nominated for a National Book Award.

A Theme of Dislocation

Thomas Francis McGuane III was born on 11 December 1939 in Wyandotte, Michigan. He is the oldest of three children. His father was a railroad laborer's son who grew up in the small town of Ayer, Massachusetts, before attending Harvard as a scholar-athlete who majored in English. Thomas McGuane II then moved to Michigan and became a successful manufacturer of auto parts. McGuane's mother, Alice Torphy, was an English major at Regis, a Jesuit liberal arts college in Denver. Essentially, McGuane grew up around books and clever talk. He sees his parents as upwardly mobile readers who were eager to secure footing in the upper middle class. Their reading consisted of the works of Fitzgerald and Hemingway, among others—"the things that could be found around semi-cultivated households in the fifties."[1] McGuane feels a closer kinship with his mother's family, who he says were the sort of Irish people who loved to tell stories. McGuane did not develop deep roots in Michigan, because his mother maintained that Massachusetts, not Michigan, was home. As a boy he spent most of his summers in his grandmother's house in Fall River,

1

Massachusetts, a house he remembers as being always full of people who valued repartee.[2]

It was here that McGuane became aware of the importance of timing and pacing. He remembers once going on too long with an anecdote, only to have his mother ask him, "What do you think of cottage cheese?" When he started to reply, she left the room.[3] The message seemed to be, get to the point, and get there fast—a point he appears not to have forgotten, for today McGuane the novelist favors short novels. Few of his works stretch beyond 200 pages. To his mind, such length is, in the nomenclature of the auto industry he grew up around, the perfect power-to-weight ratio.

Along with this love of outlandishly good talk came a feeling of being perpetually on the outside. McGuane feels that the Irish are outsiders in their own country because the English have owned everything for so long. In Massachusetts his family continued to feel like aliens in a Yankee Protestant world. When his parents moved to the Midwest, they felt not like midwesterners but like Catholics. McGuane sees this situation providing a useful consciousness: after all, "the vantage point of most authentic modern fiction is dislocation."[4] McGuane's protagonists have continued to be out of step with the mainstream, usually because of natural and honest tendencies toward the unconventional.

McGuane grew up in Grosse Ile, "a wonderful little island town that was not a suburb at all but had its own small town essence." The family looked across the water at Canada from a 115-year-old house that had been a final stop on the Underground Railroad. McGuane feels he needs to dispel the idea that he was a rich man's son:

My father didn't really do well financially until I was in my late twenties. I remember when I was 12, my mother told me that she thought we were now middle class. We make a lot of fun of the middle class now, but I remember thinking from the look on her face that she thought it a real achievement. I did have a certain class consciousness because both my parents had graduated from college. In the fifties, this fact counted for a certain sense of class regardless of how much money we had, but as a boy, I was not really different from the other kids, except that I wanted to write.

Fewer than 25 percent of his classmates in public school went on to college. McGuane recalls, "It was only because I was a behavior problem that the school principal encouraged my father to enroll me in Cranbrook," a private boarding academy in Bloomfield Hills, Michigan.

In addition to trips east to his grandmother's, he spent summers at a fishing camp in northern Michigan, fishing and reading nature books. In his own words, he "conducted a mixed-bag sporting life, catching perch and rock bass on worms, some pike on daredevils, some bass on a silver spoon."[5] His great love, however, has always been trout fishing. He also loved to hunt, especially birds, but in *An Outside Chance* he claims he was not proficient when he was 10 and has not improved, having at times to lie "vividly and recklessly" about the results of a day's hunt.[6] He also admits to being a bit of a klutz. As a youngster he accidentally left his father's 12-gauge shotgun in the campfire and burned the gun butt to within three inches of the trigger guard.[7] All such disclosures are, however, only for the sake of literature. The truth is that McGuane is "a pretty good shot," pursuing "blue grouse, rough grouse, sage grouse, Hungarian partridges, and pheasants" with a sporty 20-gauge.

His interest in hunting and fishing has led reviewers and critics to a perhaps-too-facile comparison with Faulkner and Hemingway. The more apt comparison may be that as with the elder authors, the young McGuane registered a strong interest in individual achievement. For instance, he never maintained a serious interest in team sports even though as a youngster he played a considerable amount of baseball: "It was the only team sport I could see because it has a more specific individuality about each position. It is still to me the most interesting team sport there is, much more so than faceless team sports."

Even though McGuane's father held out hunting and fishing as manly ideals, he seldom joined his son in such activities. When other adults would take young Tom out, the elder McGuane would complain that nobody but him was working for a living. But despite the mixed message, McGuane managed to spend a good portion of his formative years in the woods or on the lake.[8] Even though his father wanted to be close to his family, his continuing success in auto-accessories manufacturing took him farther and farther away. "My father hated people with money and yet he became one of those people," McGuane says. The elder McGuane was an alcoholic and a workaholic, "a man who never missed a day of work in his life."[9] McGuane sees the total deterioration of his immediate family to be the direct result: "My sister died of a drug overdose in her middle twenties [in December 1974]; my brother has been a custodial case since he was thirty; as soon as my mother was given the full reins of her own life, after my dad died [in 1976], she drank herself to death [by 1981]."[10] The family appears to have left the close-knit group established by the grandparents in Massachusetts, moved to the Midwest, and fallen apart.

The Appeal of the Writing Life

McGuane remembers wanting to be a writer from the age of 10; in fact, he remembers wanting to be a writer before he actually wanted to write any specific thing. The adventure reading he did as a child led him to believe that the writer's life was one of action and thought. Besides, he saw writing as a way of getting out of things: "I was not very good with authority . . . and I couldn't imagine working for anybody."[11] McGuane, however, did not find his writing aspirations encouraged at Cranbrook: "If anything, I was discouraged. The school was in the hands of obtuse assholes."[12] But he did make friends with his fellow student and the future novelist Edmund White. White introduced him to the "decadent" writers—Baudelaire, Rimbaud, Wilde, and Proust—and modeled the habit of serious and prodigious reading that McGuane has maintained. "I was very impressionable at the time," he observes, "and the thing that was interesting was to find out that literature could be so strange."

He also first saw Montana as a teenager in the fifties, recalling, "I worked as a cowboy—cowboy is too big a word for it: I worked on a ranch in an unskilled way.[13] I knew this was where I wanted to live the first time I ever saw it. . . . I made some money off *Sporting Club,* enough to buy my first ranch, and that was it. I never looked back."[14] McGuane's first ranch consisted of 14 acres in the Paradise Valley outside Livingston. Four trades later, his present abode consists of more than 3,000 acres at McLeod.

"By the time I was eighteen or so," McGuane explains, "I was in this swooning condition with the desire to make some stories." After the confinement of Cranbrook, McGuane failed to demonstrate the discipline necessary for college at the University of Michigan. The freedom available to him there was more than he could successfully manage, and he flunked out (0.6 grade point average). McGuane next attended Olivet College for a year to improve his grades. He praises this small liberal arts college but admits that his practical side got the better of him: "I don't know why I didn't stay there. I guess because it was such an obscure little place. Gertrude Stein had taught there. Ford Madox Ford had. I was extremely happy. There were two or three people teaching there, including the dean, who were indulgent of me in my whimsy to become an American fiction writer. The English teachers were out of this world. They let me spend all my time reading and writing."

McGuane then went to Harvard summer school and took fiction writing from Gerald Chapman, a scholar of seventeenth-century literature teaching on a summer appointment: "He was a fabulous writing teacher." McGuane remembers a conference in the Harvard Library during which he asked Chapman whether he could achieve success as a writer: "He was getting ready to go on a camping trip and was fooling with this Coleman stove, trying to figure out how it worked. He sort of looked at me out of the corner of his eye and said, 'I'm sure you can make it. You're terrific.' After that I went around feeling blessed."

McGuane next enrolled at Michigan State. There he married Portia Rebecca Crockett, who would remain his wife for 12 years. He also edited the literary magazine and first met the novelist and poet Jim Harrison. They were not, however, immediate friends: "Jim and I circled each other in those years, sort of suspicious of each other." Their legendary close friendship began after college, in the late fall of 1965, when Harrison's first book, *Plain Song,* came out. McGuane sent him a congratulatory note, and the two started communicating. At first, McGuane at Stanford and Harrison at Stoney Brook, they mostly communicated by phone. "When we discovered that we were spending a third of our annual incomes on phone bills," recalls Harrison, "we began to write letters."[15] For more than 20 years now, the two have been corresponding about the art of writing and the writer's place, sometimes as often as three or four times a week. Harrison explains: "What we have done for each other is try to keep the dream alive of being writers in the Faulknerian tradition, rather than public figures. We talk about literature as if it were vital, as if it were a substitute for religion." McGuane concurs: "Whenever we are around each other we leave with new enthusiasm to write. I rely on my conversations with Harrison to 'restore the original luster.'" Basically, the two novelists simply love reading and writing and getting together to talk. In the summer of 1988, for instance, while their coauthored screenplay *Cold Feet* was being filmed in nearby Livingston, they spent three days poring over Whitman's 1855 edition of *Leaves of Grass.* Essentially, they bolster each other to continue thinking that writing is still worthwhile. McGuane admits that at times he needs encouragement to keep writing: "Common sense tells you not to do it. There's already too much printed crap out there." Fortunately, the priestly Harrison reminds the more practical McGuane that writing is a higher calling. As if fate had affirmed their friendship, they have the same birthday—not the same year, but the same day: 11 December.

After graduating from Michigan State with honors, McGuane thought briefly of trying to become a pilot in the navy but enrolled in the Yale Drama School instead. "In some ways Yale was a complete waste of time," he says. "John Gassner taught the play-writing class, and a duller, less dedicated teacher never lived." Although McGuane's early ambition was to be a playwright, he changed to novel writing because of incompatibilities he saw in the American theater system: "It was getting to be less and less of an original playwright's theater, and more and more of the Broadway scene. It didn't fit me, and I knew I didn't want to live in the East. If you are going to be a playwright, you have to live in New York at least until your career is tremendously established." McGuane credits his training in writing plays, though, with helping him understand screenwriting.

Despite McGuane's frustration with Gassner, Yale in other ways proved beneficial. For the most part, he spent his time reading in the Sterling Library: "I felt you had to start from the beginning with the Greeks and then move on to the Russians, the French, and Henry James."[16] The surrealist novelist William Hjortsberg was also a student. The two became friends and spent considerable time rummaging around in used-book stores. "There was this incredible place outside of New Haven called the Book Barn," recalls Hjortsberg. "The big joke was the guy who owned it had a skinflint of a brother who owned a used book store in New Haven and he charged millions for books. But at the Book Barn books rarely cost more than fifty cents. Tom found a first edition hardcover of *The End of the Road*, John Barth's scarcest title, for twenty-five cents."[17]

The young men talked endlessly of the lives they hoped to achieve as writers. Hjortsberg remembers telling McGuane about a bizarre occurrence he witnessed while spending a summer in Switzerland. A climber had fallen off a mountain and died dangling in his ropes. Even by summer the ice conditions were too dangerous for a rescue party to get him down. Down in the village, the 11-year-old Hjortsberg spent his time putting money in telescopes designed for mountain viewing so that he could see the dangling man up close. When McGuane wanted to use the incident in a story, Hjortsberg gave it to him. They took creative matters so seriously that later, when Hjortsberg desperately needed the detail to end a novel, he felt he had to ask McGuane's permission. When one of their colleagues began to get published, they were crestfallen in envy: "We felt the great iron doors were closed and we were left out."

McGuane wrote the first version of *The Bushwhacked Piano* at Yale; he called it "Fire Season." When William Styron came to campus for a reading, McGuane and Hjortsberg sought him out. In the spirit of Sherwood Anderson's famous beneficence toward a young William Faulkner, Styron agreed to take their novels to Random House if he himself did not have to read them. They then went around in dire fear of hearing the "dreaded thump at the bottom of the stairs" when the manuscripts were returned. Styron's editor, Robert Loomis, did indeed turn both novels down but sent encouraging letters. "*Fire Season* should have been rejected," recalls McGuane, although he sees the experience as pivotal: "What the novel did was prove I could get from the beginning to the end. I discovered I could write two or three hundred pages of something."

After Yale, the McGuanes spent roughly a year in Italy and Spain. Ostensibly McGuane was tracing Hemingway's footsteps, developing his own movable feast, fishing, and attending bullfights. William and Marian Hjortsberg followed. Hjortsberg remembers that in Florence, Tom and Becky's rooms in the Pensione Bartolini were everyone else's favorite evening haunt for coffee and cookies, for the simple reason that the McGuanes could afford heated rooms. Also in Italy, McGuane developed a friendship with the American experimental poet Michael Palmer. What McGuane remembers most about Palmer is how widely read he was. While McGuane was more interested in the classic notions of English prose, Palmer was investigating the French new novel and American experimental poets.

At a time when his own work was "more in the mind than on the page," Palmer was awed by McGuane's ability to write with "extraordinary discipline and regularity. He had an incredible intensity about whatever he undertook. Like he has with cutting horses, he would follow a project through to extraordinary mastery."[18] Palmer also remembers that McGuane was not allowing himself to drink: "He kept himself under a very tight rein. It was like he knew he was vulnerable to disablement." Palmer felt himself energized by McGuane's love of the literary profession: "We knew we would be writers, but the question was, Of what sort? We were imagining ourselves into a life that was possible." While the year was a spirited time of literary camaraderie, McGuane sees the experience as continued apprentice time: "It was a pleasant, fairly superficial 10 months in Europe. I was writing stories based on what I already knew. I wasn't really getting anything new and wonderful out of being there."

In 1966 McGuane returned to the United States to accept a Wallace Stegner Fellowship for a year at Stanford. He does not, however, particularly value his fellowship experience: "The whole stance under Stegner was western writing. We used to sit around asking each other if our dads were cowboys and then feeling terrible because they weren't. Besides, Wallace Stegner was completely disgusted with my entire generation and really didn't have much to do with us. He really phoned in his teaching job. We were left to our own devices. It was nice to have had the money to be free for a year to write."

To add to his disappointment, McGuane the prodigious reader found that the other students were not as interested in being a disciplined person of letters as he was: "I remember Allen Ginsberg coming up in those years and talking to people and finding they hadn't read Ezra Pound and hadn't read Whitman, didn't care, didn't want to know the names. It was an illiterate age."[19] Even though he was in California in the midsixties, he ignored completely the social upheaval generated by the hippie movement. His dedication to his own purpose was so intense that he became known as "the white knight." He admits to being guilty of "a certain level of overkill in my judgment of those around me."[20]

Even though he completed another novel at Stanford, the fellowship came to an end with McGuane still unpublished. He had been working closely with William Decker, then an editor at Dial, drafting and redrafting for more than a half-year, and had fairly secure hopes of publishing a novel, a prototype of *Bushwhacked*. "I was down to it," he remembers. "I was married, expecting a baby [Thomas IV], needed to get something done." Suddenly E. L. Doctorow, then editor in chief, killed the project without explanation, sending the young author into a tailspin: "I'm not saying it should have been published, but Doctorow didn't honor the process." The matter still rankles: "I can't run my ranch that way. I can't hang my hired men out to dry by suddenly killing whatever projects they're working on." Even though he had been writing seriously for 10 years, McGuane still had nothing to show. His father had been telling friends that young Tom was teaching, but the truth was that McGuane had no marketable skill: "It was hard to get a teaching job then. I remember sending out 50 letters and only got two or three replies." He had trained as a writer, and so with no apparent options he prepared in just six weeks the manuscript that was to become *The Sporting Club*. He mailed the book to Jim Harrison and then went alone to Mexico to contemplate his future.

Camped on a beach, McGuane was aroused from his sleeping bag one morning by a fellow who appeared to be a big Mexican police officer wearing a gun: "I thought, my God, this guy is going to shoot me."[21] Instead, the man turned out to be the local telegraph operator who had been seeking McGuane so that he could congratulate him on having his book accepted. "The guy was just as excited as I was, and we went off to celebrate," McGuane recalls. Harrison had in the meantime delivered the manuscript to Simon and Schuster, and McGuane's life as a published writer began.

Living the Life of Novelist and Screenwriter

McGuane soon had an opportunity to return Harrison's favor. William Hjortsberg had followed McGuane to California and was completely frustrated with a manuscript that had circulated through 18 publishers with no sale. He decided to quit writing about things he knew and to venture forth into the unknown. "I would write just for fun, just to discover," Hjortsberg recalls. What resulted was the first 50 pages of Hjortsberg's first novel, *Alp*. Once McGuane began to sense that his friend was immersed in a new project, he pestered Hjortsberg to see the work in progress, which at that point was not even cleanly typed. McGuane was delighted, called it the "funniest 50 pages in American writing," and began insisting that Hjortsberg let him send it to Richard Locke, his newly acquired editor at Simon and Schuster. According to Hjortsberg, McGuane "wouldn't even let me retype it. And I got a contract when I didn't have any idea how I was going to end the book." Hjortsberg remembers that McGuane's greatest asset was his ability to inspire everyone "through the force of his own energy. I miss the days of dreaming about all the stuff that has come to pass. I miss the youthful enthusiasm and the endless talk of literature, hunting, travel."

Even though *The Sporting Club* brought an unspectacular advance, McGuane received sufficient payment from the movie rights to purchase his first ranch in Montana and a house in Key West. McGuane had spent a number of vacations during his teenage years in Venice, Florida, developing skill at sportfishing. He says, "I thought for a long time of living in the West Indies, but I realized, as a novelist, I didn't want to get out of touch with the culture that I was raised on, and which I had something to say about."[22] Key West attracted him because "it's a southerly town without the burden of southern history. . . . I like the fecund smell that the island has. I love to be out on the ocean: for better or worse, I'm still a sportsman and the ocean is one of the last frontiers where we can live in a civilized way next to that great wilderness."[23] In the true spirit of a frontiersman, McGuane has mastered saltwater fishing. He has studied the tides and can predict the appearance of big tarpon. Professional guides have judged him a capable guide.[24]

McGuane thus began the rhythm of alternating between Florida and Montana, writing, fishing, and competing in rodeos. *The Bushwhacked Piano* and *Ninety-two in the Shade* easily flowed from his disciplined attention to his calling. The world, however, soon began to become a bizarre place for the white knight who lived only to read and write. Livingston became the new artist's colony, with Tom and Becky as the focal point. Richard Brautigan, William Hjortsberg, Sam Peckinpah, Warren Oates, Jeff Bridges, and Russell Chatham were all visitors who decided to secure homes in the area. Harrison was frequently in and out. Jimmy Buffet wrote and slept in McGuane's barn. The atmosphere was highly competitive and charged with alcohol and other drugs.[25] When Elliot Kastner offered McGuane a movie contract for *92 in the Shade,* a highly publicized life of dissipation was under way. By the end of 1977, McGuane had dissolved his marriage to Becky and engaged in affairs with actresses Elizabeth Ashley and Margot Kidder, among others. His relationship with Kidder resulted in a brief marriage (from August 1976 to May 1977) and a daughter, Margaret.

McGuane attributes an accident he had with his 911 Porsche outside Dalhart, Texas, in 1972 as the springboard to the manic life he led in the midseventies. Driving at 140 miles an hour, he lost control and ricocheted off an old ranch pickup. Although he escaped unhurt, he couldn't talk: "I kept thinking I had died. I kept thinking about all the things I hadn't done."[26] At this point, McGuane assessed his life and decided he had been working too hard: "I had been so determined to be a successful writer, so sure it took insane dedication, that from twenty to thirty I did nothing else but read and write. In Key West after the accident, I finally realized I could stop pedaling so insanely, get off the bike and walk around the neighborhood. The changes that came were irresistible, but it was getting unthinkable to spend another year sequestered like that, writing. I just dropped out. I quit fighting my way through marriage and the Sunday *New York Times.*"[27]

While McGuane was directing *92 in the Shade* in Key West, John Dorschner of the *Miami Herald* commented that McGuane entered the movie business just when he should have been giving attention to securing his reputation by writing the big book: "McGuane is now at an awkward stage: no longer simply 'promising,' he is still not 'established,' in the way that . . . John Updike or Philip Roth are [*sic*] established."[28] McGuane, however, voiced commitment to the movie industry: "I have the fantasy of doing both novels and movies, and doing both seriously. If I have nightmares about that, it's because I know no one has done it. If I knew of someone else, I'd feel a little bit safer."[29]

In order to direct *92,* McGuane had to promise a British production company the talents of Peter Fonda and Warren Oates. McGuane worked for free; the actors, for less than their usual fee. The main drive behind McGuane's desire to direct was the usual screenwriter's complaint of not wanting to turn one's work over to other people. The other films that carry McGuane's name as screenwriter do not appear on screen the way he conceived them. *Rancho DeLuxe* is missing scenes that illustrate McGuane's insight into contemporary Indians, the ending for *Missouri Breaks* was redone by Robert Towne and Jack Nicholson, and *Tom Horn* was rewritten, in kindly fashion but still rewritten, by Bud Shrake. *Cold Feet* received a massive preproduction rewrite by McGuane himself.

McGuane's hopes for himself as a cinema artist, however, were not what interested the media about his life and career. At the height of the film years, the *Village Voice* published a piece depicting McGuane as too self-consumed, too wide-eyed in Babylon, and hopelessly incapable of making objective judgments about his life and work. The article's writer, Michael Tolkin, allows McGuane to make a fool of himself. Tolkin begins by setting him up as a literary naïf in Hollywood. Speaking of *92 in the Shade,* Tolkin says: "McGuane wrote the novel. McGuane wrote the script. McGuane directed the movie. In one grand gesture he has ripped off a chunk of every English major's wettest dream."[30] McGuane is quoted as saying that he has always thought of the movies as some sort of "Jewish black art," and the reader gets the impression that he can't really believe he is to be part of the magic kingdom. Still, he doesn't seem to think he actually is part of the literati. After casting aspersions on English professors and the New York literary establishment, McGuane adds: "I am exhilarated by the crassness of [the movie] industry. . . . I'm bored to death with the elitism of experimental writing. . . . There's no business in writing books. . . . Making money is a lot of fun."[31] To this day McGuane feels called on to defend himself against the piece: "It was an unbelievable setup. Tolkin had to give me directions to the Brown Derby, then he made it sound like I hung out there all the time. My comments about the Jewish power structure were directed toward the homogeneity of the business. I was saying that I felt like a stranger in a fraternity where I really didn't speak the language."

Tolkin goes on to point out that McGuane's movie days are on the decline. The people with power do not like *92,* and *Rancho DeLuxe* has been released only in the Midwest. McGuane's only hope resides in *Missouri Breaks*—which did go on to fail at the box office. Tolkin depicts McGuane being puzzled by a *Variety* review that calls the *92* protagonists white trash. McGuane claims not to understand the review, because he too is white trash. Tolkin quickly points out that McGuane's father is rich, evidently the crowning evidence that McGuane doesn't know who he is, that he is out of his depth in Hollywood. Tolkin fails to note, however, that the story's protagonist, Tom Skelton, is also rich and that trashy behavior among the well-to-do is a favorite target of McGuane's humor.

Tolkin then proceeds to focus on the upheaval in McGuane's family life and the pointlessness of his relationship with Margot Kidder: "McGuane stood a few steps back from her, arms crossed, paternally surveying this girlfriend whose agents are tearing their hair out while she sabotages her career to be the 'bimbo' of a great director-to-be. Maybe."[32] The article ends with McGuane, the seemingly rugged frontier writer, worrying about whether he has what it takes to become a success in Hollywood. He admits, for instance, that it is hard to get to direct and that after he finished the final cut on *92* he was so anxious he had to hurry home to Montana and vomit blood.

Michael Palmer remembers thinking that McGuane had allowed himself to become trapped in a hopeless situation: "Tom had always thought like Hemingway: throw the manuscript over the fence to Hollywood, take the check and walk off. All of a sudden the dynamic became too complex for him. I say this nonjudgmentally since a poet has the luxury of going unread."

In a 1985 interview, McGuane demonstrates a more objective viewpoint about writing for the movies:

I remember thinking what a pale experience it was compared to writing fiction. At first it was rather frightening, with all these people around and a lot of equipment and a lot of power tripping going on, but then soon it had become as if I were trying to say something with this extremely ungainly typewriter. I kept thinking over and over, this is so much less good than writing fiction, because I'd get an idea and then I'd have to move all this junk around to shoot it, and then by the time I did that, inertia had set in again. . . . There's not much room for innovation at the process level. At any rate, I don't think I'd want to direct again.[33]

The problem is that McGuane has found Hollywood money necessary to remain unfettered in order to write serious work. Screenplays take McGuane about six weeks to write and earn as much as six times more than a novel that takes two or three years to create.[34] Even though *The Bushwhacked Piano* received favorable reviews, was featured in the *New York Times,* and won the Rosenthal Award, McGuane's income from the hardcover edition was only $3,700, obviously less than he could possibly live on. As he explains, "It's very hard to earn a living on the kinds of things that one did when one was Stephen Dedalus."[35]

McGuane continues to vacillate about writing for Hollywood, saying, "You only have so many silver bullets. I'm trying not to dissipate my writing energy." When it is a question of simple human relationships, he enjoys the work: "They are some of the hardest working, brightest, most talented people I've ever been around. You go out there and you have warm companionship among your fellow workers." But he continues to be ambivalent about the stigma common to writers of his generation that screenwriting is some-

how a debasement of his gifts: "To be perfectly honest, I think writing novels is a more important thing for me to do. In terms of my usefulness on
earth, it's a higher degree of usefulness for me to figure out how to write
these unremunerative novels."[36] At the same time, McGuane's inclination
toward Hollywood stems from his practical sense of self-reliance: "I survived
till I was 41 before I had any outside help. I don't want to become complacent. The main thrust of my family's income must come from my writing."

Reshaping the Writing Life

McGuane's concern that he might become complacent derives from the
financial security he engineered after becoming heir to his father's business:

In 1981 when I was 41 I was suddenly the owner of a company. I had a lot to do. I
had more income—income I had never had before. I was immersed in a world that
was kind of like the world of Quinn [in *The Sporting Club*]—the one he was escaping from. I was running back and forth to Michigan or Atlanta. It was kind of fun
after my mother died because we didn't have to do things cautiously for fear of losing her income. I had an income; I didn't have to worry about going completely
broke, so I made some sort of reckless—not reckless, but bolder—decisions about
what to do than we had been able to do before, and we ran [the business] for five
years. We sold it last spring for six or seven times what it was worth when my dad
died.

In September 1977 McGuane and Laurie Buffet, the sister of rock-and-
roll singer Jimmy Buffet, were married, and McGuane began to achieve a
fulfilling family life. But first his writing life had to sink to its lowest ebb,
which it did with the publication of *Panama,* his fourth novel. At the time
McGuane considered it his best work. Like Chester Pomeroy, his protagonist who spirals from sudden and outrageous fame to complete disaster with
no one to blame but himself, McGuane had decided to reveal certain truths
about himself. When a number of reviewers panned the novel, McGuane
resorted to alcohol with bitter self-destruction.

Slowly the world provided by Laurie and her daughter, Heather, and the
soon-to-be-born Annie, brought McGuane around to realizing how good
his life really was. In 1981 he gave up alcohol. He explains, "When you
drink a lot, your ego is exacerbated by the process. You are in the fray in
terms of the elbowing that goes on between contemporaries. When you quit
drinking, you get more contemplative about life. Someone charges forward
and says, 'I'm the best writer in Montana.' Now I say, 'That's fine. You can

be that.' I used to say, 'No, you're not. I am.' But literature is not a form of warfare."

McGuane's current life is remarkably more sedate than in the midseventies. He lives almost reclusively, writing, working his horses, and tending to ranch chores. He remarks:

I'm genuinely happy. I really like what I'm doing. I'm really enjoying fatherhood at all levels. I'm having a great relationship with my son. My son is so much like me. He used to tilt at windmills. I spend a lot of time telling him what I've sort of found out. He's getting more contemplative.

My little girl is great and my two other girls—Heather is a student, a real achiever; Maggie, who lives with her mother, and I are getting caught up. I didn't see much of her in her early life. I don't have the continuity with her, but we are both aware of that and working on it. She and Annie get along real well and are inseparable when she comes out here. We're all close. My wife is a highly motivated, energetic person. We get along well. So if I'm going to take time away from them it should be something that is important to me.

McGuane sees the wonder of his own childhood reawakened in Annie, from whom he has rarely been separated since she was born. He feels he is seeing with fresh eyes: "One of the things I'm learning through Annie is the female view of the world. It is not the same as boys; it is a nonconflictive, nonevasive kind of play. She seems mostly to see pleasure in the world. She is so new."

On the ranch, McGuane raises, breaks, and markets cutting horses— those used to separate nonproductive or injured cattle from the herd. Cutting is also a contest event, and McGuane animals have earned numerous Montana, Pacific Coast, and national titles. The McGuanes also own from 20 to 25 brood mares. Spring through fall, McGuane spends about five hours each day on ranch work. Seven or 8 mares drop colts in the spring. He trains cutting horses and tends to necessary tasks, such as mending fence. Each summer the McGuanes feed 150 head of cattle for sale in the fall. Given an ideal day, McGuane would like to read for three or four hours every morning: "My personal list of things I feel I should have read, all those things that make me feel less than prepared when I sit down as a writer. . . . I think you should expect a writer to be a true man of literature—he should know what the hell he's talking about, he should be a professional."[37] He prefers to write for three or four hours after lunch before returning to ranch work until dinnertime. Evenings he prefers to spend reading.

The most useful aspect of ranching for McGuane the novelist is that it keeps him among nonliterary people: "I spend a lot of time with cattle feeders and horse trainers and breeders and ranchers, and I like that."[38] McGuane's pedigree as a rancher is not exactly authentic, but he does take satisfaction in the knowledge that veteran stockmen accept the McGuane ranch and its breeding program: "People around here have strong opinions about what constitutes a good cow."[39] Experience, he asserts, is the true novelist's business; he feels a necessity not to lose touch with those who unselfconsciously move through the natural flow of life: "We've all seen these nameless, faceless people out there, and when we track one of them back to wherever they came from we sometimes find that this is the one person who can pull a breach-birth calf without ever killing the mother cow, or the guy who goes over the hill and does beautiful fencing even though nobody is watching, the valued neighbor who will get up in the middle of the night to help you get your water turned back on."[40]

This respect for people has kept McGuane from seeking or accepting any sort of patronage from the academic world. His fear is that the result of living one's life securely within a college English department would be a great homogenizing and narrowing, thereby eliminating the sinew from his fiction. He prizes writers like Norman Mailer and Walker Percy, those "who report to us from the whole world."[41] And as a writer who has managed to survive via screenwriting, he sees writers who rely on the academy as greatly underworked: "Just because you're not making a living from your writing does not mean you have to become a teacher. I've had miserable writer-teachers; they thought they were of purely totemic value sitting at the head of a class monosyllabically reacting to students' questions."[42]

In keeping with this distrust of the academy, McGuane has no interest in experimental fiction for the sake of experimenting:

At this point in my life the writing that I really like has clarity and earned and rendered feeling as its center. Writers who have done that most successfully leave you feeling experientially enlarged, rather than awed or intimidated—those things which have been the basis of the modernist response in writing.[43] Readers are generally quite smart. They have real instinct about what is based on personal knowledge—what is real, what is true, the kind of observation that is based on deep personal knowledge and experience that is exactly translated into language. There's a world of literature out there that has this quality of really counting for something in a very exact way. Turgenev's sportsman's sketches, Hemingway's short stories, the early Steinbeck. You have to design automobiles based on what people want and what they need. And you have to write books the same way. It's not pandering to the market; it's capturing human nature, the basic human family. When you strike those moments of truth in writing, it's exactly the same wherever you find them. The reader says, "Oh my god, that same thing is true of my aunt Harriet." You feel a flowering from your stomach through your mind. All serious writers are struggling to find those moments of recognition of the human condition.

McGuane considers Montana his adopted home. He is attracted to its "dopey complacency" and the plethora of hard-bitten romantics still in love with the Old West.[44] "The air of the fresh start is alive here," he maintains. "People are willing to accept the idea that you can pull your life out of the fire and turn it around completely."[45] Even though he does not want to be thought of as merely a regional writer, it is important for McGuane to feel himself a part of the glory that was the Old West. He is proud of his time spent "jackpot roping"—the team roping championship at the 1977 Gardiner, Montana, rodeo is his most publicized victory—and especially of the thumb he maimed at the sport: "Some cur said I had *writer's hands,* which really got to me, as I am someone who wants to be a rugged guy in the West and not some horrid nancy with pink palms."[46] In 1989 McGuane received the Montana Governor's Centennial Award for Literature. He sees the award as a degree of acceptance from his adopted state: "It means more to me than the National Book Award would have."

McGuane no longer ropes competitively, because he began to notice that the roping stock was occasionally injured in the process. Even though he still helps out at brandings, he prefers to expend his energy on the cutting horse contests, because they do not hurt animals and because the drama involved in the responses of a good horse appeals to him: "When you train a horse, you have to imagine what the horse sees, you have to react the way the horse reacts." Horses, as well, seem to provide McGuane's life with a special kind of stability:

With horses, I feel I've discovered some ancient connection, as though in some earlier life horses were something that mattered to me. The close study of all animals teaches us that we're not the solitary owners of this planet. As my horses procreate, and as they search for food and companionship and try to grow up and face one another's death, we see these things and it's very moving. . . . I don't know what that has to do with how we own the earth and own the universe, but in a way I feel religious about it. It's not an accident that there are these sentient creatures other than human beings out there. And we're not supposed to populate the universe without them. We're seriously and dangerously deprived every time we lose one of these animals.[47]

Perhaps because he is a transplanted midwesterner, McGuane wants to empower his fiction with the energy and essence of Montana: "I've struggled to have a sense of place. . . . I do think you can use nature to charge a fictional landscape with powerful results. I have no interest in replicating Montana or rendering landscapes in a recognizable way, but I do know there is something forceful about these landscapes that should turn up in language."[48] Nor does McGuane see his fiction as a place to replicate his own life. Personal events serve only as points of departure: "Art is there to be served and we go where that's supposed to go, not where the paltry details of one's life might dictate." Autobiography is "a place to sort of lift the edge of the material so that I can enter."[49]

The world McGuane chooses to enter is the dislocation of the contemporary West. In his view "the West is a wreck."[50] Things do not necessarily change for the better just because people have westered and achieved the American dream on what was once the American frontier. As people accumulate wealth, the pace of life accelerates beyond sanity. They run errands in helicopters; they jet around the world buying the best-bred stock; they amass an array of items for no other reason than that they can afford them. They become controlled by the out-of-control pace of their lives: "All of a sudden they are up against the accumulated values of the civilization to that point, but they have to deal with them because money, drugs, speed and airplanes have brought them to a point of exhaustion."[51] Eventually, contemporary life becomes a matter of simple survival within a complex and unfathomable matrix.

McGuane's foremost challenge here is to capture the confused congestion of life. He credits Gabriel García Márquez, Günter Grass, William Faulkner, and Herman Melville with achieving such feats but worries that in comparison, his own work may be rather thin: "My biggest problem with the novel is whether or not I'm producing a sturdy enough tissue for that tension, since it's so miserably low in its lows and in its highs it approaches goofiness. I'm trying to find a way to avoid trivializing the serious stuff without undermining the comedy of it."[52]

In his daily writing, McGuane sees himself as an explorer. He prefers not necessarily to know where the writing is going: if he has a clear objective in view, the outcome will be too limited. He is not only the writer but also the first reader, eagerly awaiting the surprises of the story. A 200-page published novel will spring from an original draft of 600 or 700 pages, which will require numerous drafts and revisions. McGuane says that when the writing is going well, "there is an element of real, deep-down excitement about the process. It is the harder way to write a book, the wilder way."[53]

McGuane compares himself to a bird dog initially receiving a strange and strong scent: he must run, sometimes in circles, until he finds the exact nature of the pursuit. Echoing Henry James, he explains that sometimes this process begins as a single image or a picture around which characters begin to move and language begins to form:

I believe Charles Olson's old dictum that writing should be one perception leading to another perception. And when you start to do that you can't write very fast and you can't think about the big book. You just have to do that dirty work. Tough, mean work. Sometimes it means you have to live more or think more or try harder. You just have to say I am going to do it this way, wherever it leads. You become a totally uncommercial entity. On the other hand you have the opportunity of communicating in a way that is more satisfying than anything else that happens.

Once the characters begin to act out the story, McGuane the author keeps his options open. He allows the characters unlimited freedom to pursue varied possibilities. Even though he outlines every project before he begins, the covenant he has with himself is that he will revise and redraft to whatever lengths are necessary. The original outline is usually the first thing discarded. He is not troubled if the writing seems interminable; possibility rather than closure is uppermost in his mind. "Wasted pages" are a normal part of the process; blind alleys help to propel the outcome.[54] This procedure frustrates his friend Harrison, who changes very little because he thinks about his work for long periods before he begins to write: "McGuane revises too much; he excises too much great material."

As McGuane reflects on the current stability in his life, he remembers a time that he and his father visited a neighbor's bomb shelter in the fifties. The elder McGuane began immediately pondering whether he, too, should build one for his family. Then he said, "I think we'll just stay up on the ground and take our lumps."[55] Like his protagonists, McGuane has taken his lumps and survived, and he is confident that he will continue to develop as a human being and an artist from whatever adversity the future may hold: "I think that life kind of hurtles forward in a massive way for the world, but within it, people invent islands—islands of sanity, islands of family continuity, islands of professional skills and power, islands of craft, art, and knowledge. Those islands basically are contributors toward a cure for despair, in ways that we probably cannot quite understand."[56] As McGuane views the world from his island, his motivating "vision of excitement is to be able to read and write harder."[57]

Chapter Two

The Sporting Club: Rivalry and Comic Violence

Overview

Thomas McGuane wrote *The Sporting Club* in six weeks, in the wake of his disappointment from the Dial rejection of the prototype of *Bushwhacked Piano*. He did not plan or outline or attempt to salvage previous material: "I just sat down and rolled the paper into the machine and put '1' in the right hand corner. And I never have done that again." *The Sporting Club* concerns the destruction of the *Centennial Club*, the most ancient and distinguished of rod-and-gun clubs on Michigan's Northern Lower Peninsula. The club, chartered in 1868, has provided summer relaxation and recreation for generations of the upper-middle-class pretentious. The club's traditions of self-satisfaction and self-aggrandizement finally overwhelm Vernor Stanton, an unstable and violence-prone young man who refuses to accept the responsibilities of adulthood. Through a series of deft moves, Stanton engineers the infighting necessary to bring about the demise of the club, which finally occurs when a photograph unearthed from a time capsule shows the first generation of club members engaged in a sexual circus involving not only all manner of human anatomical perversion but also animals. The inhibitions of the current members melt away, and they begin to fornicate perversely in the manner of their ancestors.

Pivotal to the success of Stanton's scheme is his old friend James Quinn, who formerly shared Stanton's passion for making the world an uncomfortable place for the conventional and inflexible. Both men are heirs to millions, and although Stanton has never held a position of responsibility, Quinn has recently taken over the management of his family's auto-parts factory. To Stanton's dismay, Quinn enjoys the work. In fact, Quinn realizes that the old life of adolescent high jinks with Stanton was actually boring. In their school days they were constantly committing crimes against the social order and competing with each other to see who could be the most outlandish. Stanton's current version of this competition is to continually challenge Quinn to a duel with French pistols and wax bullets. Quinn always loses, each time coming closer to serious injury. As the plot unfolds, Quinn, against his better judgment, is more and more drawn into Stanton's scheme, and in the penultimate stages of the novel actually joins in the destruction of the club.

Critical Reception

The Sporting Club appeared to a chorus of positive reviews from influential critics in impressive places. In the *New York Times Book Review,* Joyce Carol Oates called 28-year-old Thomas McGuane "that notorious and difficult creature—a writer of promise."[1] *The Sporting Club,* she asserted, was another in the brilliant line begun by Bellow in *Henderson the Rain King,* the new genre of the paranovel that on the surface resembles the traditional novel but in actuality deals with characters who are not really real and whose job it is to show how exaggerated, silly, and tedious life really is. Oates sees the tall tale and outrageous events of the novel as Faulknerian. Even though she thinks the novel promises more than it gives and has trouble taking the moral outrage of the satire seriously (something she has just said readers are not supposed to do when reading a paranovel), she concludes that McGuane's comedy "is engrossing and at times ingenious" (5).

John Leonard, writing for *Life,* begins his review by invoking the presences of Hemingway and Fitzgerald. Leonard credits McGuane with insights into competition and money that go beyond those of these two famous literary fathers. Leonard's one negative note is that he cannot accept the pornographic photograph. He thinks McGuane is attempting to demonstrate that corruption is inherently human, rather than a consequence of human actions. Even though Leonard feels the photograph is a humorist's trick that weakens the book, he concludes, "It is the only stumble in this extraordinary first novel."[2] Giving McGuane brief notice in the *Nation,* Sara Blackburn says the novel reminds her of *The Great Gatsby* and finds the author "one of the most interesting young novelists to have appeared in a long time."[3] Linda Kuehl in *Commonweal* calls the novel a "dazzling accomplishment."[4] The London *Times Literary Supplement* finds the book a parable about America and McGuane's language dashing and Joycean.[5]

McGuane's first published effort, then, yielded comparison with Bellow, Faulkner, Hemingway, Fitzgerald, and Joyce, giants in their generations. Joyce and Fitzgerald are dazzling sentence makers. Bellow, Hemingway, and Fitzgerald are all midwesterners. As McGuane's career develops he will become more and more conscious of his upper-midwestern roots. In fact, at one point he says, "A midwestern childhood is going to show. . . . Sooner or later someone looks into your eyes and sees a flash of corn."[6]

A Reading

The wholesome connotations to the values inherent in this "flash of corn" are the focal point of *The Sporting Club*. Themes centered on friendship, work, and commitment beyond oneself emerge from the text. The story is limited to the point of view of James Quinn, who is beginning to think like a responsible adult. Stanton is frustrated with Quinn for outgrowing the need for freedom and frolic. Although the two protagonists spend most of the novel in disagreement with each other, they exemplify the values that will be apparent throughout the McGuane canon.

Quinn is discovering how unfulfilled he is when he is not home running his auto-parts factory. The truth is that Quinn values work. He is a calculator who thinks things out. When he begins to work in his father's factory, the first important assignment he receives is organizing the company picnic. He goes about the task systematically, interviewing employees so that he can understand their exact wants, and auditioning bands so that he can be certain they will play the exact music his people desire. Since a number of his employees are handicapped, he takes pains to see that they will feel included at all times. It is important to note here that even though Quinn may have enjoyed making the world a tense place for strangers—for society in the abstract—when he is confronted with the needs of human beings whom he knows individually and who have placed their faith in him, he is sensitive and kind. Because of this systematic preparation, the employees have a wonderful time at the picnic and Quinn is a success. Once he takes control of the factory, he is just as systematic about the daily affairs of the operation. Even when he is on vacation, he is in constant communication with his secretary and has his work mail forwarded to the club daily. What is important here is that Quinn is crucial to the factory and therefore draws his meaning and well-being from his work.

With Quinn the systematic approach is actually a Hemingwayesque code that he follows in all endeavors. For instance, he wants to be a sportsman of gentlemanly cast. When he fishes for trout he "dresses for fishing"[7] and is constantly casting and moving "carefully" (25). Tasks must be done right, with respect for correct technique and ritual-like procedures. He even eats oysters with style and grace (67). McGuane is both serious and satirical here; real Hemingway-code heroes adhere to more significant rites— maintenance of dignity, grace under pressure—than consuming oysters

properly. That Quinn should be code-oriented is humorous, yet his systematic approach is admirable. He is a person in whom others can place their
trust; he understands and fulfills his human responsibility to achieve nobil-
ity no matter how mundane the task.

This concept of code adherence is epitomized in Jack Olson, the club
groundskeeper and guide and a native of the upper peninsula. In fact, it is
his people—there are Olsons too numerous to count in the phone book—
whom the original club members swindled to get the land. Olson, unlike
the upper-middle-class pretentious, is a natural and authentic sportsman.
Even though his equipment is not expensive and his dog is without papers,
his respect for the appropriate processes of sport is such that he constantly
outhunts and outfishes the members. Quinn respects this native and natural
talent.

Stanton, however, shares none of these code concerns with Quinn. He
wouldn't think of defining or developing himself in any sort of work. He
demonstrates his contempt for the one job he did have—in a company he
owned—by urinating in a potted plant in the executive lounge. When
Stanton pursues game, his only concern is to bag the best and the most; in
whatever arena he must come out the victor. Essentially, he is "an odious
apostate" (64). When Quinn, Stanton, and Olson go midnight fishing,
Quinn and Olson demonstrate respect for the fish, the river, and the
weather. Stanton, however, simply thrashes about killing fish, and with a
storm brewing, keeps the others out too long to ensure their safe return.
Stanton has no respect for Olson as a man who reveres the earth. That there
might be a sportsman's code that demands respect for a process larger than
satisfying his own desires is beyond Stanton's understanding. He is a total
isolato; he has respect for no one. In his self-absorption and disrespect for
land, animals, and people, Stanton appears to epitomize all that is spiritu-
ally corrupt in the world of sport.

Even though Stanton does not respect the working-class Olson, he is
thoroughly bored with the supercilious pretensions of the club members.
Whereas Quinn can coexist with the club even though he knows much of its
ambience is phony, Stanton cannot, because his sense of outrage at what is
phony requires that he thoroughly frustrate those who are self-satisfied.
And the only way he can be certain he has made his point victoriously is to
totally destroy the Centennial Club.

Here, then, is a distinct difference in the controlling romantic spirits of
these two men. While Stanton is a self-absorbed bully, Quinn is basically
concerned with doing right by people. He sees himself as a serious code
hero. In his reveries he often casts himself as a savior—a cowboy or a knight.

For this reason Quinn values the simple farmers who live around the club. He despises the way the club continues to encroach on the farmers' lands and thereby put an end to their rustic existence. He sees basic human value in the way the farmers live their lives, getting from and giving to the land. By contrast, Stanton's favorite reveries deal with the Middle Ages. He is very much a nobleman; peasants are there for the taking and the abusing. That Olson's family has been on the land for generations means nothing to Stanton. In fact, he is not even willing to allow Olson caretaker status on the land from which he sprang; he instigates Olson's dismissal in order to commence the chain of events that leads to the club's demise. Stanton is an evil knight who swears fealty to no powers higher than himself.

Earl Olive, Olson's replacement, is an example of the characters Joyce Carol Oates feels are not actually real. Olive is a former live-bait salesman—that is, he dug up worms and sold them. The people Olive surrounds himself with are fat, ugly, and dumb. They ride motorcycles, fornicate publicly, and generally behave as if gratification were a divinely inspired guiding principle. Like Stanton and his primitive obsession to dominate, they live on a bestial level. They are, if anything, perhaps too real, too earthy, to blend nicely with the pretensions of the club members. The club members, in turn, are too concerned with proper form. They pledge allegiance to the traditions of the club, which appear to be nothing more than snobbish preoccupations with their own importance. The members fascinate themselves with club history, collections of toy soldiers, and sentimental attachments to past amusements. As Stanton says, "they sit around and pick each other's noses and read the *Wall Street Journal*" (132). Both social groups, McGuane seems to be saying, are devoid of any meaning—if meaning comes from self-fulfillment in the service of a higher order, as it does for Quinn in his factory and the trout stream.

Meaning for Stanton seems to come from violence. Whenever he is thwarted—as he is when he thinks Olson condescends to him and when Quinn refuses to help destroy the club just for the fun of it—he demands a duel with French pistols. Even though he uses wax bullets, he all but dismembers Quinn, who never lands a shot. Stanton's way of dealing with Fortesque, the club bore, is to engineer a situation that leaves him tarred and feathered. Such preposterous violence will remain a strain in McGuane's work. It is a part of the inherently human corruption that John Leonard cannot accept in McGuane's work. Human beings seem to deal too harshly and unthinkingly with one another, but such behavior is germane to the paranovel concept Joyce Carol Oates cites. Violent behavior in *The Sporting Club* is not of itself sickening. That the novel is predominately satire and the characters not always round helps blunt the thrust of much of the violence. There is a sort of cartoonish, pratfall tone to most of it. When the situation becomes serious, as in the duel with lead bullets between Stanton and Earl Olive, two semiround characters, the slapstick disappears and Stanton and Olive refuse to shoot each other. After the duel, Olive attempts escape and even though the club members subsequently subdue him through genuinely frightening mob violence, the comic tone ultimately prevails. As Olive is conveyed along, his ankles and wrists bound to a pole, he explains "what a letdown this was in his life" (215) and destroys any semblance of tragic mood.

The idea of a romantic love relationship with an unattainable woman will become more complex in McGuane's work, but in this first novel women seem to exist mostly as sex objects or as support for male-determined agendas. Although Quinn has two sexual encounters during this summer at the club, he remains unfulfilled. The first encounter is with Lu, a voracious teenage motorcycle enthusiast who rolls Quinn "like a cloth window shade" (128) but has little personality and no inclination to limit herself to him. McGuane's Lu is mostly a male fantasy of the willing conquest. Quinn's attraction to her is a matter of appearances; her breasts are called "yummies" (123) and her legs are suggestively dimpled. She too measures Quinn singularly by his appearance and is attracted to him because he's cute. She is an expert at the sex act in which she engages solely for physical pleasure. Quinn need not feel any sense of obligation or guilt, for she is clear in explaining to him that he is not "Mr. Right" (129).

The popularity of sex for sex's sake seems to cut across class divisions. While Lu is of the lower class, Quinn's other sexual encounter is with a handsome young mother who is a member of the club. When they first meet at the club beach, they glance at each other knowingly but do not speak. Later in the novel they encounter each other in the shadows and begin aggressive foreplay almost without introduction. In fact, the woman does not speak until Quinn has completed his orgasm and then she only tells him not to stop. When he does stop, she berates him. Like Lu's, her interest in sex is physical. She demonstrates no awareness that Quinn is a human being and not a sex object.

These women are free, independent beings, certainly, and there is no indication that they in any way subordinate themselves to Quinn. But as characters these women are not driven by a very full psychology. They are exactly like Quinn's secretary, Mary Beth, who struts around the office making outlandish bids for sex until she is certain Quinn is not interested. Then she satisfies her physical urges with salesmen, accountants, and file clerks (100). Her only concern is sating her physical needs. And Quinn sees her only as a possible sex object; before passing up an opportunity, he gives some thought to enjoying sex with her. Quinn is not really forced to confront these women as people. He may want to be loved but not actually by any of them. They exist, then, not for themselves but as good-time girls for men who want unemotional sex. We do not, for example, see that these women have actually developed a sexual philosophy; we see only that they are ruled by their physical needs. They are clear examples of the early McGuane female, women whose requirements are decidedly physical and who exist essentially as figments of male fantasy.

Stanton, like Quinn, appears to desire an authentic love relationship. But "love" to Stanton appears to be of the one-dimensional, storybook variety. He falls in love with Judy, the aunt of his current companion, Janey, on first sight and offers her the world and everything he has. He carries on, Janey explains, like a "poor lovesick baby" (187). This episode is an ironic twist on the suffering of unrequited love. Stanton, though he pines miserably, has no intention of worshiping Judy's chastity from afar; he is mostly concerned with the frequency of her intercourse with himself and others. Judy, like the women in Quinn's life, has no fully developed psychology.

Janey, the main female character in the novel, appears to be self-reliant but is actually quite subordinate to Stanton. She lives and travels with Stanton but will not marry him. Even though she admits to regretting that she loves him, Janey, in the manner of a sound appendage, will not leave him. She does not approve of his obsession with making the world tense or of his expensive guns and boats. Stanton abuses her in public but in private showers her with affection. She is not docile but stands up for herself and talks back to him. Because she is constantly showing Quinn pictures of the people in her life before and after Stanton, relationships seem to hold great meaning for her. But just why she remains with Stanton rather than embarking on a life of her own is a mystery. The traditional response that she loves him is evidently sufficient cause for her willing subordination. Indeed, self-assertion on her part is met with the retort "hang up the jock," which would indicate that Stanton's only definition of a self-actualized woman is a woman who attempts to act as a man (29–30).

Stanton and Quinn have very different attitudes about Janey. Stanton admits to loving her but also refers to her as a "piece of ass" (74). Quinn, on the other hand, romanticizes Janey and his role in her life. He feels he must protect her from Stanton, that she can't possibly know what she is getting into. When he begins to sense that Janey does not need his help, Quinn is somewhat irritated with her. He does not want his women, he realizes, to be in control of their situations; rather, he wants them to need a prince to rescue them. Quinn, it seems, is not ready for a self-reliant woman.

As the novel ends, Janey is in "crazy control" (185) of Stanton's entire existence, even to the point of cuing his utterances. Ultimately, then, she is stronger than Quinn—and even Stanton—can acknowledge, but she is still living her life as an appendage to a man. Her role in the novel is to be first Stanton's companion and then his nurse and manager. Even though she is strong, she is not free of the traditional woman's role of caretaker to males. That Janey is willing to accept such a role as right and proper seems to turn entirely on the fact that she has a physical attraction to Stanton she cannot overcome. Underneath her strong exterior, then, beats the heart of a subordinate, rather than that of a full-blown, self-reliant woman.

Much of the novel's comic texture comes from McGuane's ability to provide the well-crafted phrase and the outlandish tale. The author appears to be a raconteur attempting to outdo himself. For example, when Quinn is extricating himself from the collapse of the club, he indulges in an interior monologue that includes "I must have freedom and it is only that which will do. The swamps breed discontent and therefore bomb all moist places. Wendell Wilkie and the clear plastic tears of Mexican virgins implore you to sink giggling beneath consideration until all the beasts of the zodiac raid your poor brain. Remember that help yourself is a novel of please and that if you try too hard you will be seen to the door, your mind belly up and your hat in your hand. Life's a greedy railroad and that's an end on it" (209). All of which seems to be saying that in order to survive without compromising, one must be careful not to try too hard. Meaning here, however, is beside the point. Cleverness exists for its own sake.

In the same vein McGuane provides a magnificent history of mooning, an adolescent and outlandish strategy of Stanton and Quinn to unnerve the staid world. The art moved from simply exposing one's buttocks in public to flattening them against a slow-moving car window ("the press") and then to the ultimate fame reserved for those who mooned pursuing police officers. Stanton and Quinn, of course, turned the art into a contest and tried constantly to overexpose each other. Eventually they took to daring feats of mooning while on foot, a practice that led to their arrest, jail, and lifelong roles as suspects in the investigation of sex crimes (179–81). Ultimately Stanton decoys the authorities with fake pornography, sues for false arrest, and wins. The entire passage has the feel of stories good old boys tell one another while passing the jug in a liar's contest. McGuane establishes himself here as a master of hyperbole, the stuff of life to loquacious Irishmen. This mastery of the art of entertainment sets up an intertextual tension in McGuane's work. It is difficult to be ridiculous and profound at the same time. Broad comedy and satire are amusing, but they do not earn their authors the respect accorded the ironic and the deep. As his later work demonstrates, McGuane's concern for "showing off in literature" has lessened as he has matured.

Parental and ancestral influence, as well as intergenerational conflict, all of which will become paramount in McGuane's mature work, makes a minor but significant appearance in *The Sporting Club*. One of the points of the sexual circus depicted both in the pornographic photograph, in which Quinn's great-grandmother participates (202), and in the rapine nature of the club's past is that one's ancestors are corrupt. Given Quinn's and Stanton's propensity for outlandish behavior, McGuane seems to be asserting that human beings cannot rise above corruption in the blood.

In many ways, Quinn and Stanton seem to have the same parents, beings without apparent impact, serving only as simple springboards from which the protagonists leap to define themselves in the vacuity of contemporary existence. The mothers are the subordinated sort whose codes of conduct revolve around the home and the conventional expectations propounded by fashion magazines (23). The fathers are upper-middle-class industrialist achievers who conventionally tend to business. Quinn's father fears retirement (49). Stanton's father is oppressive and ridiculous (42), quite unable to understand his son's idiosyncratic frustrations with conventional life. Quinn's father is also ridiculous; he thinks golf is a dangerous game (50). Both couples are boozy (164, 176). The alcoholic parent and the effects of alcohol and other drugs on parents and protagonists will become a stronger force in McGuane's work. In addition, the outlandish Stanton and the practical, work-appreciating Quinn will develop into a single protagonist who embodies both qualities and is consequently at war with himself.

Ultimately, the novel makes a moral point, namely that the haves in the United States have continued to thrive at the expense of the have-nots. Initially, government agencies were bribed by club members in order to clear the original homesteaders and loggers from the land (147). Ways of life supported by minor prosperity came to an end so that the upper middle class could play at rusticity. And much to Quinn's dismay, the Centennial Club has continued to buy up bordering family farms, in effect driving the indigenous population from the area (79). Proclaiming the club ancestors to be a "swinish pack of human refuse" (204), Stanton implores the current membership to join him in praying for the bomb this country so richly deserves. Nothing short of annihilation will stop the abuses people are capable of committing on one another. This point is brought up again more seriously in an exchange between Quinn and the tarred-and-feathered Fortesque, who illustrates the plight of those who live by appearances. The tarring and feathering has left Fortesque diminished in his own eyes, and he cries openly in front of Quinn. His main concern is not that Quinn be compassionate but that Quinn tell no one he witnessed the crying. Though Fortesque in his heart of hearts knows that the picture he presents to the world is a facade, he is incredulous when he sees the facades of others destroyed. Seeing the club members and the surrounding townspeople going berserk with sexual perversion and violence, he implores Quinn to tell him that the world isn't like this. "I think it is," Quinn responds, and moves on (213).

Americans, the novel asserts, are living in a time when the only values are acquisition, subordination, and self-gratification; values with human empathy at the core seem impossible to maintain. At one point Stanton retrieves a one-horse sleigh from the bottom of the club lake. Later, after the lake is drained by an explosion, Quinn comes across the skeleton of the horse. The horse is stretched out like an arrow (169), recalling the American 1950s, when persons of integrity, persons who acted for right above self, were called straight-arrows. Quinn mounts the skeleton and in his mind rides the horse into the sky, the stars trailing behind him (170). He appears to have had a moment riding Pegasus, as if he were some sort of Pecos Bill, some sort of transcendent hero. Quinn seems to understand, however, that such symbols of rightness no longer exist to inspire humanity toward lives of truth, justice, and fair play. Later he says, "If wishes were horses. If all the pieces were a whole" (209). The pieces, however, cannot be a whole. The romantic hero, the prince Quinn wishes to be in saving his lady love, has no impact in our time.

As the novel ends, Stanton has gone completely insane, suggesting that one cannot dominate or change the flow of human history all by oneself. Stanton now owns the club, but Janey and attendant mental health professionals only allow him to think he's in control. Quinn, on foot instead of horse, has taken refuge in his factory, a smaller world not entirely within his control but at least one in which he can systematically achieve an impact. They are, the novel's final sentence explains, "compromised and happy" (220). Happiness, then, can become a viable substitute for mocking established social orders with outlandish behavior when such happiness derives from work the protagonist imbues with meaning. In McGuane's later fiction, his protagonists will realize that the enemy is not represented by the pretentious persons of the parental generation and the ignorant of one's own; instead, it derives from an uncontrolled need to abandon conventionality and attempt to find meaning outside the self. The more recent protagonists will at least begin to understand that they must forge their own meaning and produce their own happiness.

Chapter Three
The Bushwhacked Piano:
The Protagonist at Large

Overview

The Bushwhacked Piano is the culmination of work Thomas McGuane had been attempting to unify for years, and the novel contains material that predates *The Sporting Club.* "I wrote out of a desire just to be funny, to make people laugh," McGuane says. The novelist trained on picaresque structures from Daniel Defoe to J. P. Donleavy to Saul Bellow: "It was pure open road comedy." The American Academy named the novel recipient of the 1971 Richard and Hinda Rosenthal Award, given annually to the best novel that sells the least. Arriving in New York to receive the honor, McGuane felt completely out of place: "I remember standing in a group of these writers, all of whom I recognized, and I thought I should introduce myself because everybody was standing there sort of glumly. John Updike was staring at me. After a couple of minutes he said, 'We don't even know who you are.'" The young McGuane perhaps too confidently responded, "You will."

In *The Bushwhacked Piano,* protagonist Nicholas Payne is more fortunate than Quinn or Stanton. At the novel's end, he is uncompromised and happy. He is McGuane's Nick Adams, but he is less passive than Hemingway's young man. While Nick is often unwillingly victimized by experience, Nicholas seeks adventure by assaulting the power of the conventional life. As a child he actually bushwhacked—shot and destroyed—a neighbor's piano. His father has the finest law practice in suburban Detroit and wants Payne to join the firm. But Payne has no intention of doing anything "the tiniest bit regular or respectable."[1] He wants "fun" (120) out of life; he hunts ducks and journeys on his motorcycle while his father talks of enemas and profits. Payne wants no part of his father's "declining snivelization" (50) and "the pismire futilities of moguls" (128). Because he has sensed his own mortality from the death of a wisdom tooth (12), Payne wants personal fulfillment rather than upper-middle-class success, adventure rather than mundane work. And because he is a traditional picaro, Payne remains undeterred in his quest.

Payne also desires Ann Fitzgerald, an aspiring poet and photographer whom he, creator of his own life that he is, sees "almost as a goddess" (44). But her parents, Duke and Edna, "social figments of the motor money" (21), think Payne shabby. The respect of their social peers, hard work, and achievement mean everything to them, and Payne doesn't measure up. But Payne is not concerned, because their lives are uninspired and his wanderlust is the same as that which spoke to such nonconformist American heroes as Jack Kerouac and Twain's Huck Finn. The Fitzgeralds transport Ann from Michigan to their ranch in Montana, but Payne follows, imagining a transcendent adventure involving "himself and Ann in some cosmic twinning" (46). Movement appeals to Payne, and so does the romantic idea of an almost-unworldly mate. In his mind, he is remaining open to possibility by living without regard for the boundaries of upper-middle-class life.

Ann, however, is also sleeping with an establishment boyfriend named George Russell, who has a more-than-promising future at General Motors. Still, the would-be artist in Ann is attracted to Payne; she thinks experience with him could "expand her spiritual resources" (102). For this reason, she is in charge of her feelings and their relationship. She sees in Payne a "romantic fragibility" (102) that seems to mean "childlike vulnerability" that results in real emotional losses; these she envies because she knows nothing will happen to her that she can't outgrow. She simply does not want to grow up just yet but will stay with Payne until she has nothing to learn from the relationship.

Lasting fulfillment with such a woman is impossible for Payne. She will not give up George completely, because she knows someday she will have to behave like a conventional adult. But for now, camera in hand, she joins Payne on an expedition to Florida to sell fraudulent bat towers, a scheme Payne is involved in with C. J. Clovis, a multiple amputee with a surreal vision of America. In reality, Ann accompanies Payne because she is too much under the influence of her own naive romanticism; she thinks she will discover the essential America by experiencing common people. At one point she slows up their trip just to play country music on a roadhouse jukebox and dance with "a really unpromising collection of South Florida lettuce-pickers and midcountry drifters" (167). Such a seedy milieu is evidently required for an awareness-expanding experience. In the end Ann feels "a grave seepage of idealism" (203), leaves Payne for a boatload of shrimpers, and her adventures concluded, marries George, the two of them becoming the "perfect monads of nullity" (218), comfortable within the security of conventional society.

McGuane accentuates Payne's estrangement from society when he offers a review of Ann's first photography show. The reviewer sees in the group of pictures entitled "Nicholas," a "vision of what is lost in the conventional life" (219). The reviewer labels Payne's life banal and sees Ann's photos as "a cautionary monument to the failed life" (219). We understand that those inside the conventional life will never understand Payne. To strive outside normalcy is to be banal and failed, yet Payne will not relent. He feels he has "put it all together at a time when life was cheap" (220)—a time when conventionality will not allow him to be who he wants to be and therefore must be ignored. Payne's movement outside mundane spheres will not cease. He is, for better or for worse, in charge of his own life, the artist of his own destiny. A life lived against the ordinary ends of conventional society requires great faith in the self, and Payne manifests the necessary resolve.

Critical Reception

The critical response to *The Bushwhacked Piano* was strongly favorable. Important notices came in the form of essay-reviews in *Saturday Review,* the *New Yorker,* and the *New York Times Book Review.* The last publication also carried a photo of a smirking and apparently cocksure 31-year-old Thomas McGuane. Evoking the ghosts of Hemingway and Joyce, J. D. O'Hara, in *Saturday Review,* finds the novel remarkable because even though its basic premise is not new, McGuane's rendering is mostly funny, sometimes eloquent, and always "fast-moving and inventive."[2] O'Hara is deeply taken with the young author's ability with well-turned phrases and crazy characters. McGuane's craftmanship, O'Hara asserts, is the real reason the thesis that the fully realized life is lived outside conventional society is convincing. The reviewer's one serious criticism is that Ann, as a character, is "sandbagged by the exigencies of the plot" (49).

In the *New Yorker,* L. E. Sissman, too, comments on the lack of originality in the novel's premise but credits McGuane with "joyous inventions in the present tense."[3] McGuane's stereotypical characters actually sidestep stereotype because of his "all-American insistence on pushing an idea to its ultimate and revealing absurdity" (124). Sissman credits McGuane with sharing Céline's genius for viewing the mundane materials of daily existence as an organized nightmare bent on eradicating any trace of humanness from life. The reviewer's main concern is that McGuane overwrites, hammers home his points with "unnecessary obviousness" (126). He cites the scene in which Ann and George Russell are reunited, Ann capitulating to George's standing offer of marriage, and argues that readers can see plainly the conventionality of the two characters; McGuane need not refer to them as "perfect monads of nullity." Sissman, however, forgives the excess because McGuane is a young writer "blessed with an abundance of power" and praises the novel for its invention, freshness, language, and "persuasive argument that in these days the death of youth is the death of life in America" (126).

Jonathan Yardley begins his *Times* essay by explaining that McGuane is a "writer of the first magnitude" and "a talent of Faulknerian potential."[4] In fact, Yardley invokes Faulkner's name five times in the first five paragraphs. Yardley sees McGuane as being in the mainstream of American literary tradition, but unlike Faulkner, who saw the human race enduring all catastrophe, McGuane is more skeptical: his characters are "venal, exploitative, irrevocably corrupt" (6). Human beings will not triumph; they will simply accommodate. Yardley also finds McGuane's women to be shallow. Still, he states that *The Bushwhacked Piano* is the best picaresque novel since Bellow's *The Adventures of Augie March* and commends McGuane for his humor, his language, and his perceptive social criticism. Yardley's one serious complaint concerns what he refers to as McGuane's condescension to middle Americans. McGuane's portraits of ordinary people, Yardley thinks, are mere caricatures, a serious flaw because given McGuane's "extraordinary gifts, all he needs is to care for his people as much as Faulkner cared for his . . . , and his work could well be . . . of comparable excellence" (18). Yardley implies that McGuane, after two novels, has fallen just short of greatness.

A Reading

The Bushwhacked Piano is intellectual exercise, the cerebral vision of a precocious young writer. Demonstrating little empathy with the human condition, McGuane goes for verbal wit; his characters are there to be manipulated through ridiculous antics. Little if anything in this vision is sacred. The center is not holding; in this absurdist dream of contemporary America, things move too fast and discrete entities lose the fight for individuality. The world is without foundation. Ultimately, then, the novel provides a look at pretensions that motivate contemporary American life. McGuane lampoons upper- and lower-middle-class stability, self-conscious artiness, and most clearly the myth of the quest for America—the road and the territory, as it were, immortalized by Jack Kerouac and Huck Finn.

The schema, of course, revolves around Payne. He is right in revolting against the status quo represented by his parents and the Fitzgeralds, but he is also pointless because he knows from the beginning that his rebellion against the established order and his quest for Ann are doomed. Yet true to the absurdist and existential soul that motivates both self and vision, he quests anyway, for he believes, as does McGuane, that beneath the seeming craziness of a life without foundation there is an authentic America. By the novel's end, however, we have only a vague notion of what that authentic America might be.

At the same time, we achieve a somewhat clearer notion of what this authentic America is not. We can be relatively certain that it is not the secure suburb provided by Payne's parents. Yet the picture given of the protagonist's parents is not necessarily bad. Essentially, they want their son to get a job, to begin a productive—conventionally productive, but productive nonetheless—life. His parents are offering Payne a place in his father's office because that is the one thing they can offer. It is important to notice here that they are offering rather than demanding. When Payne's father pesters him to fix the breakwater that keeps the Detroit River out of the lawn and the basement (38), he is actually trying only to get his otherwise-useless son to do something constructive around the house—to earn his keep, in Old World parlance. The elder Payne is also acting to protect his home—not exactly a reprehensible motivation.

The Fitzgeralds are more completely drawn and are laughably shallow but not clearly insidious. Their concern is for their own and Ann's safety. They are motivated by fear. They can imagine no other sort of existence than their own, and Payne simply frightens them. The wig bank, owned as an investment by Mrs. Fitzgerald, is an indication of their superciliousness. The ranch, an investment for Mr. Fitzgerald, the managing of which he knows nothing about, indicates how far away they are from the authentic America in which Payne believes. Their primary concern is financial security, a not-altogether-un-American urgency. Nevertheless, these pampered denizens of corporate America, with their unquestioned courses fixed and staid, are hardly examples of the adventuresome and muscular American heroes celebrated by such writers as Kerouac and Walt Whitman. The two sets of parents here are not so much evil as they are superfluous to Payne's vision of the fully realized life.

The lower-middle-class persons, seen most clearly in the Floridians who purchase the fraudulent bat tower, are simply less secure versions of their financial betters. Dexter Fibb, who is grand master of the Mid-Keys Boosters and in love with symmetry, and the U.S. Navy chief petty officer, who berates his wife's interest in celebrities and keeps the secrets of the public address system to himself, stand as fine examples of the myopia of middle America (209–14). For them, order is the ultimate truth. Both men have survived and defined themselves by complying with the demands of the systems provided for them. They have by nature no understanding of a person like Payne, who wants to live outside the system, or Clovis, who wants to exploit its fragility. The system allows middle Americans a secure existence of sorts and is therefore sacred. The failure of all such systems, as far as the Paynes of the world are concerned, is that systematized life precludes adventure and possibility. Ultimately, Payne, a would-be Pecos Bill (66) bent on transcendent adventure, simply has no place to realize himself.

Another subculture McGuane satirizes is that of American machismo. Interesting here is that McGuane as an author is often criticized for sexism and a Hemingwayesque maleness, yet in this early work demonstrates that exaggerated virility is more often than not the main characteristic of hapless bullies. Wayne Codd (in addition to meaning "food fish," the word *cod* also refers to "a husk"), the Fitzgeralds' new ranch foreman, is a swaggering cowboy without internal substance. Even though Codd blows himself up to his full height in the best movie-cowboy fashion and threatens Payne with fisticuffs, Payne, who gives his own masculinity hardly a thought except as it relates to the sex act, fells Codd with little effort. After Codd assaults Payne with a sash weight (not exactly a macho instrument), Codd retreats and confesses (admitting the Fitzgeralds put him up to it) readily enough when faced with that most ordinary of horrors, a lawsuit. He appears not to understand his own tight-lipped macho code.

The other ridiculous macho character is Doctor Proctor, a former fighter pilot who "amputates" Payne's hemorrhoids. Proctor, who has developed no sense of self-worth beyond the glory of his war days, knows who he is only when he is in his trophy room. Longing for his fighting past, he survives by taking drugs. He is totally bewildered while operating on Payne. He has forgotten surgical technique; he cannot control his coordination; and he botches Payne's operation. A macho hero of the highest military order, the man is entirely incapable of fulfilling his civilian responsibility.

The crowning ignominy for machismo America is that neither Proctor nor Codd is good with women. Their real relationships are with themselves. Codd situates himself under the bathhouse floor and takes photographs, for later use alone, of Ann's vagina. He also sits in a tree and watches Payne and Ann cavort in her room. Such pressure is too much, and he resorts to onanism, spending his seed on the roof. Similarly, Proctor walks around his trophy room making little wrist-flicks at himself and visualizing his nurse naked. In America, it seems, to burlesque Hemingway, real men live without women.

The neutralizing power of the myth of macho violence is seen when McGuane, borrowing from Mark Twain, has Payne disperse a mob of drunken shrimpers bent on a gang rape of Ann. Payne and Ann are in a motor home parked outside a bar, and the shrimpers continually harass them until Payne goes outside with a revolver. Since he is dressed only in undershorts, he is not an imposing figure, and the mob utters the conventional B-movie remark about not pulling a gun unless he intends to use it. In fact, they do not find him intimidating until he jams the gun in the leader's mouth: "They could tell that Payne had reached that curious emotional plateau that did not necessarily have anything to do with anger that, once gained, let one man kill another. Payne would never have known until he had done it" (175). This final point is underscored later when Payne tells the bar owner that he will kill people if he and Ann are harassed again. The bar owner turns white, even though Payne is merely indulging in hyperbole.

What makes these scenes interesting is that Payne is not the one acting with macho bravado. The shrimpers are the tough guys; they do physical labor, talk tough, wear tattoos. Payne is simply acting to protect the sanctity of his "home"—albeit the arrangement in this case is a very brief one. Payne acts from basic human instinct, while the threatening shrimpers—as well as the swaggering Codd—act from an empty concept of reality, one that does not provide them with the confidence necessary to be effective in normal life. Like the townspeople Colonel Sherburn so easily disperses in *Huckleberry Finn*, underneath their bravado they know that their own macho-inspired strength is phony and that they are easily frightened. They are in a sense victims of their own belief in violence because they don't know that all macho-inspired strength is phony and they actually seem to believe Payne is the genuine article. Because Payne does not view himself that way, the entire concept of macho superiority betrays itself as false.

Ann's commitment to art for art's sake is another pretension the young McGuane cracks open for a closer look. In essence, the novel has much to say about the manner and place of the serious artist. In the style of satire, the text seems not to explain where exactly genuine artists come from, but it does illustrate that the genuine artist is not like Ann, that is, one who decides to appear to devote herself to art while at the same time refusing to risk her upper-middle-class security. Like the D. H. Lawrence referred to in the novel, Ann is a self-conscious artist, bent on romanticizing experience. This quality is what attracts her to Payne; she knows from the beginning that their relationship will not achieve fruition and that in the end she will return to the corporate fold by marrying the safe and secure George Russell. We know that Russell is not "real experience"—whatever that means in Ann's mind—because like Codd and Proctor, he is not good in bed, a world where Payne excels.

It is Payne's own self-conscious nonconformity that attracts Ann to him. Ann knows that the part of her that is attracted to Payne is not the real her. When she and Payne go to Florida to install the fraudulent bat tower, she peroxides her hair, paints her nails, and tries to feel like a "hoor" (161). She cannot really give herself over to Payne's lust for adventure, because she needs to feel she is in charge of their relationship at all times. For instance, at one point she does not want Payne to know how clever she is (145). Art, we are led to believe, is her real quest, as she photographs Payne relentlessly.

For Ann, art is not something that can grow from the genuineness of her inner being; rather, it is an adventure she must go out and find. Art is something that cannot be generated by her real self; it is something she must dress down to create. The novel makes this point rather harshly when Ann travels to Galveston with the shrimpers. Her adventure is handled in mock-epic tones. She is doing "Galveston by sea" (182), a phrase that would lead us to believe something considerably more elegant than a short run on a shrimp boat is happening. Of course, a lot more is happening: Ann is "committing experience" (204). *Experience* here is a lofty-sounding, Lawrencian word for engaging in group sex with the shrimpers. The concept of "true art"—art that grows from genuine experience—is ravaged in the hands of would-be artists like Ann. The point is made more emphatic when her photography show is reviewed and the shrimpers seen in various stages of undress are given credit for exhaustion at the end of a difficult day, when in fact they are lining up to take their turns. Inauthentic experience produces sham art. Ann is a "monad of nullity" (218) here because the essential thing about a monad is that it cannot be influenced; an untrue artist, she is not receptive to the wisdom experience might bring. Her quest for great art comes down to nothing more than a fling in preparation for a secure marriage.

McGuane's treatment of Ann could be read as detrimental to women, but his purpose is larger than the denigration of females. In fact, no one, including Payne, is treated any more or less reverently than Ann; everyone's foibles seem to be exposed. In Payne we see what happens to those who self-consciously quest, in the manner of Kerouac, for America. When the novel opens Payne has already gone on one such quest. He has motorcycled cross-country and found America to consist of various guises of lunacy (12). The reason Payne is impatient with Ann's Lawrencian sense of the oneness of things is that he has seen nothing in America he wants to be at one with. Yet the myth of America is stronger than the realities Payne has discovered, and he voyages again, this time in a green Hudson Hornet. Payne knows his quest is an act (16, 174), and his choice of a vehicle long out of production supports the idea that he is after a grail that no longer exists.

It is easier to see the America Payne does not want than to understand what the young quester hopes or expects to find. He wants no part of upper-crust Detroit, a West in the hands of absentee landlords and swaggering cowboys who dress like Nashville singers, or middle Americans who survive by allegiance to systems. Even the Ann he loves is a construct of his imagination. He knows she respects power most of all, but he ignores her real self for the momentary purposes of his search. Like C. J. Clovis, he seems to know the country is a giant crap game (91), and for the time being he is content to roll the dice and trust blind luck, however outrageous the results might be.

Payne's dilemma can be seen in his two favorite artists, Paul Klee and Norman Rockwell (140). Rockwell's well-known *Saturday Evening Post* covers depicting the everyday scenes of a supposedly bygone era in American life illustrate the sort of human fiber and strength Whitman thought he saw in the American people. On the other hand, the work of the Swiss expressionist Klee seeks to capture the mystery of existence through a mixture of observation and intuition. For Rockwell, the surface details carry the story; for Klee, details evoke underlying ideas, the relationship between viewer and viewed continually dynamic. Rockwell is sentimental; Klee, witty and bizarre. And there is Payne: a sentimentalist seeking the witty and bizarre.

This ideal exists in Payne's relationship with Ann. He does feel that they should be able to build a relationship on love alone—after all, togetherness is really all he has to offer her. It bothers him as well that the glitzy America resides on ground once inhabited by American Indians, a people who, at least in mythology, coexisted with the earth rather than brutalizing it. Though Payne is amused by the middle-American Floridians, in the end he respects their essential goodness to the point that his conscience will not let them be swindled and he admits publicly to being a con man—an act so outrageously honest that his victims do not know what to make of it (213). They seem so unused to human honesty that they are actually more comfortable suspecting him of being a sham than they are knowing he is one for certain.

His friendship with C. J. Clovis is another thing Payne takes quite seriously. We know from Clovis's surreal signs depicting the disintegration of America (44, 91) that he and Payne are soul brothers, and this brotherhood forces Payne to think in terms of something more noble than simply generating outrageous fun. When the hypochondriacal Clovis, who has already lost an arm and a leg (a wonderful literalizing of the cliché) trying to survive in America, enters a Florida hospital convinced he is about to die, Payne agrees to submit to the hemorrhoid operation so that he can be near his "dying" friend. As things turn out, there is nothing wrong with Clovis and Payne sacrifices his rectum (risks his behind) in the service of friendship. And finally, as the bat-tower scam erupts in climax, Clovis dies in Payne's arms. The scene is both a satirical version of the surrogate-father tableau from B movies and a Rockwellian sentimental act at the same time. The fact is that his human bonding with Clovis matters to Payne, a young man for whom hardly anyone or anything has meaning.

For midwesterner Nicholas Payne, then, love, empathy, and friendship still have validity despite the America he finds himself a part of. Finally, it appears that Payne will not find the America he wants, the America of the open road, of honest possibility and adventure. If America is a lost cause, what, then, of Payne? The novel ends ambiguously. In fact, Payne may actually be approaching insanity, because he appears not always to know what is real and what is not. But given the America of the novel, he need not worry about what is real, because unreality seems a way of life for almost everybody. And the indications are that it will continue to be a way of life for Payne. Ready to spread peanut butter on bread with a jackknife, he stands on the shore looking out to sea:

The sky rose over him, round and vitreous, a glass enclosure. He smiled, at one with things. He knew the great blenders hummed in state centers and benign institutions; while he, far away, put it all together at a time when life was cheap.
But then the abrasions, all the incredible abrasions, had *rendered* him. The pale, final shape of Payne, like the yolk of an egg held to the light, had come to be seen.
I am at large. (220)

Payne's spreading of the all-American food with the all-American utensil illustrates that he has not given up on the country, or its possibility; the only enclosure is the sky—and by extension, the universe. And despite his dislike of Lawrence, he is at one with the universe. He has put it together, determined who he is and that life has value in spite of prevailing absurdity. He has learned all this because of the pain of confronting the various guises of the system, but this abrasive endeavor has brought his sense of himself into clear focus. And this knowledge gives him confidence to carry on with his quest. As Payne stands contemplating the sea and the sky, the Hudson Hornet awaits departure, pointed at the interior of the continent. Payne may be contemplating the sea and the sky, but his commitment is to earth. If Whitman's and Kerouac's America with its unique possibility is still out there, Payne will find it. If not, he will thrive on the search.

Nicholas Payne is a young person's protagonist. But he is neither Huck Finn nor Holden Caufield, because he is neither naive nor bewildered. He is innocent in that he appears unaffected by experience and, satire aside, sustained by belief alone (104). He acts as if a fully realized, self-created life is possible in America. He vows that systems of established order and disorder will not influence him. He will be Payne and compromise with nothing; he will continue to bushwhack pianos. Only the young maintain energy for such a quest. As the McGuane protagonists mature, they will become more exhausted and less definite in their objectives. Payne's quest for possibility will become tempered by the later protagonists' inability to rise above cultural absurdity; they will fall victim to brooding sadness, a fate of which Payne is only vaguely aware (178); and movement will become less and less consoling, their quests for meaning appearing to be more of a running from than a running toward experience.

Chapter Four

Ninety-two in the Shade: The Discovery of a Life

Overview

Thomas McGuane knew he was capturing the ironies of American life when he was drafting *Ninety-two in the Shade:*

I had been in Key West fishing a lot. One day I was going along and I saw this giant billboard with a picture of Egg McMuffin and I thought, Is this what America is? I began to wonder if I could go on. I remember feeling I was in a kind of cultural earthquake that somehow I was part of. As I wrote, I could feel the cultural reso- nances humming up through the keys of the Olympia. It's the only book I've ever felt that. I felt I was in a parade. It was written in a fairly straightforward way. I felt it was cinematically, surreally structured. Juxtapositions, voice changes and so on. I was thinking more in terms of blocks than in a narrative thread way. It was different than anything I've done before and different than anything I've ever done since.

Ninety-two in the Shade, set in Key West, a "Hotcakesland" of American consumerism, concerns Thomas Skelton's quest for fulfillment. Skelton feels a fully realized life will not be possible for him unless he is out on the ocean guiding fishing tourists in his own skiff. Even though he prepared for a career in marine biology in college, his life has been mostly pointless drift- ing. A thorough student, he analyzes Nichol Dance and Faron Carter, the two most successful guides around. In the end he chooses to emulate Dance, a renowned long-shot artist. Dance respects the young man's abilities but doesn't think the tourist traffic can support another guide. Attempting to discourage the young fanatic, he plays a joke on Skelton, sending him out to guide the Rudleighs, an upper-crust couple. Dance hopes that Skelton will decide against spending his life with such ersatz sportspeople. Their whiny self-absorption is so antithetical to Skelton's code of sportsmanship that he releases a trophy fish Rudleigh has caught. When Skelton discovers that the entire affair is a joke, he burns Dance's skiff in retaliation. The outraged Dance vows to kill Skelton if he insists on becoming a professional guide, but Skelton goes into business anyway, because his self-fulfillment depends on it.

Like Nicholas Payne, Skelton does not want to be swept along in the flow of life; he wants to sense that he is living life his own way. The fear of death cannot stand in his way, because "there are no tremendous deaths any more. The pope, the president, the commissar all come to it like cigarette butts dropped to the sidewalk from the fingers of a pedestrian hurrying on toward some cloudy appointment."[1] The situation here is much the same as in the earlier McGuane fiction. The protagonist must assert himself against the conventional flow of life, which is essentially empty and too much determined by the crassness of American consumerism. With his life in danger, Skelton ought not to guide, but to do less is to lend "yourself to the deadly farce that surround us" (166). McGuane makes clear that "the deadly farce" is inevitable when human beings absent themselves from vital energies and capitulate to the purposeless machinations of ordinary life. In the manner of an adolescent, Skelton transforms the idea of "having his own way" into a cause célèbre. Skelton must stand up for the self he desires to be and quest for the life he wants.

Unlike Nicholas Payne, Skelton is not alone in his idiosyncratic, if not self-aggrandized, desire to fulfill himself. Family and friends seem to care about him, although they are not always understanding about his goal. His father and grandfather, two genteel outlaws, worry about his safety and wish he would not attempt to guide, but they do support him. His grandfather, Goldsboro Skelton, has earned millions from dealing with crooked politicians. During World War II, his father ran guns and his own whorehouse, from which he married Skelton's mother. Exhausted by contemporary life, Skelton's father sits in bed all day. At night he roams the streets in a bed sheet, looking for women. In addition, Skelton's girlfriend, Miranda, does not want him to risk his life guiding, but she lends her support, mostly by bringing him to multiple orgasms.

Ninety-two in the Shade is a decidedly complex work that could be considered McGuane's most optimistic book were it not that when Skelton becomes a fishing guide, Dance kills him. Until this very end, Skelton seems to have everything going his way. He has determined his own values and his own fulfillment. He has the support of family and a rewarding love relationship. But he also has his feud with Nichol Dance, who shoots "him through the heart" (196). McGuane ends the novel by explaining, "It was the discovery of his life" (196). Skelton's discovery is that despite his having the courage to pursue his dream and the conviction to withstand adversity, life is "not theater" (196). Life does not come equipped with happy endings and, McGuane seems to be saying, will pierce you in the heart. Fulfillment is neither long lasting nor ultimately completely possible.[2]

Critical Reception

Ninety-two in the Shade was widely and favorably reviewed. Almost all the reviewers mentioned McGuane's two earlier novels, contrasting themes, protagonists, and plot elements with *Ninety-two*. All proclaimed the young author's third novel not just an improvement on the other two but a work that demanded a serious reader's attention. They seemed to be saying, Here is a writer up to the challenge of telling us the truth about ourselves. Hemingway's presence was continually invoked, probably because of the themes of male competition, macho bonding, and commitment to an unstated but mutually understood code of masculine behavior. In addition, because of his eye for the absurd in American life, McGuane was often compared with Mark Twain.

A consistent observation, usually made too adroitly to be considered severe criticism, was the notion that McGuane's sentences might be overpacked with cleverness. More than one reviewer singled out Skelton's thought that "facetiousness can be a way of dancing at the edges of the beautiful; it can also be facetiousness" (107). When the young McGuane is at the top of his form, he dances on the edge of the beautiful, unquestionably, but he is also capable of showing off with words to the point that some reviewers found his clever constructions vague. In fact, Walter Clemons, in *Newsweek,* finds a blank at the center of the book because the notion of masculine affection depicted in the Skelton-Dance relationship is too abstract. Clemons, however, does say that *Ninety-two* is "a very fine book" and that McGuane is "a saturnine virtuoso moving . . . toward mastery."[3]

The landmark notice came in the *New York Times Book Review.* Here Thomas R. Edwards offers a useful insight into McGuane's characters: McGuane's heroes are young men with family and money behind them. They need not take the exigencies of daily life as seriously as do their lower-middle-class counterparts, who must, for better or usually for worse, accept life in the plastic and neon "Hotcakesland" of a consumer-goods America. McGuane, says Edwards, has trouble writing "sympathetically about people who fall short of his own intelligence, intellectual sophistication and toughness. His bright, cool, ironic, literate young heroes . . . respect only men like Nichol Dance, quiet, capable out-doorsmen unspoiled by culture, given by

Nature to know what college-boy types can only gradually learn by think-ing and suffering."[4] Edwards suggests that simpler people may be seen from the inside to have a pathos all their own that is unknown to the aristocratic eye. He also points out that McGuane could hold a more empathic view of women, although he thinks Skelton's mother and Jeannie Carter are im-provements on the female characters in the earlier novels. Still, the overall tone of the review is positive, and Edwards concludes that McGuane "is an important as well as brilliant novelist, one of our most truthful recorders of a dreadful time" (2).

Invoking the Hemingway mystique, the *Time* review by Martha Duffy is titled "Papa's Son" and begins by stating that McGuane is a descendant of the days when the purpose of fiction was to render the essence of experi-ence. Duffy points up comparisons with Hemingway (style, linear details, and, though in not the same words, "grace under pressure"—Heming-way's idea that the protagonist, when confronted with adversity, should maintain his own code of integrity) that are supported by the young novel-ist's seeming willingness to assert that all serious writers owe Papa a debt of one kind or another. Duffy concludes that McGuane is very strong and that *Ninety-two* is his best book yet.[5] L. E. Sissman, in the *New Yorker,* calls McGuane "a more modern, more ironic Hemingway,"[6] and without specifically mentioning the master, chides McGuane for pompous didacti-cism stemming from his need to solemnly share life's profound lessons once he has learned them himself. Sissman concludes by declaring *Ninety-two in the Shade* a signal of what is to come from McGuane's "steadily burgeoning talent" (89).

In the *Atlantic,* Richard Todd finds McGuane a gifted young writer but wishes he would try something other than to keep alive themes he has inherited. Todd, unlike the other reviewers, reserves his verdict on McGuane's future: "I suspect the test for McGuane will come when he sets out to create a man who is not lighting out for the territory but trying to find his way into other lives, other heads."[7] Todd seems to be treating the author like a young Huck Finn. Todd's message is simple: life must be lived not on the river but on the land; create characters who engage the world rather than run from it. Indeed, since *Panama,* McGuane protagonists have attempted, sometimes in rather idiosyncratic ways, to engage the world but have met more often with failure. Still, in the later work, McGuane has deepened in wisdom and begun to shape a clearer and more personally human vision of life as it is and can be lived in America.

A Reading

Ninety-two in the Shade is protagonist-centered fiction. It is also concerned with the possibilities for survival in a world in which the guidelines are unclear and the conditions for upper-middle-class life unappealing. Thomas Skelton is in the process of creating his own life, of generating his own meaning. He is helped in this process by the knowledge that his own family is unconventional; he is also hindered because he seems to have no real foundation from which to build. Unlike the earlier McGuane protagonists, however, Skelton is aiming at something concrete. He is not interested in making conventional people uncomfortable (*The Sporting Club*) or in finding Kerouac's America (*The Bushwhacked Piano*). Instead, he wants to make his own place in the America that is available to him, but the task turns out to be more difficult than he thinks it should be.

The text opens with Thomas Skelton wandering under the influence of drugs, and we begin to understand what McGuane means by his use of the term *Hotcakesland*. Human life is without backbone; people exist without purpose; the republic is in trouble, and nobody seems to know what to do about it (3). The cause seems on the surface to be the residue that appears on the edges of capitalism: pollution, land development, an anything-and-everything-is-for-sale brand of commercialism. The real problem is at once simpler and more complex: life has no personal or collective meaning. Finding meaning, then, seems to become a process of elimination. In the early going, Skelton walks away from drugs and guns. Despite the ease with which hallucinogens and violence are turned to, they have no impact on the prevailing despair. Skelton fails both to achieve personal fulfillment and to establish an understanding of collective worth. The novel provides no clear vision of the worthiness of contemporary life.

Skelton also feels that his family has been lost to him (15). As he wanders through his parents' empty house, we cannot be sure whether (a) they once were a family in the conventional sense and such traditional warmth and support is what he senses a loss of or (b) they were never close and the customary existence is a valuable experience he feels he has missed. Whatever the case, the concept of family does not provide him with meaning. He puts his faith in Miranda, until he discovers her romping nostalgically with an old lover. Since she is "his" girl, he is troubled. The romance of commitment, a rule he seems to be counting on, has just become indefinite; a prescribed code of behavior seems not to be holding true. Relationships are supposed to mean something, but precisely how loved ones are to have meaning is not clear to Skelton.

Skelton's concern with Christianity suggests that he feels life's ultimate meaning should be spiritual. He scoffs at a Christmas manger scene made of plumbing parts but admits that the simple faith it depicts is his own (37). Unfortunately, a simple faith will not sustain Skelton in the Hotcakesland of our time. By conventional standards he has lapsed in the faith, but as Saint Matthew instructs, Skelton is willing to make his own hellfire (56). Such an endeavor requires that Skelton test his faith (122) and in the process invent his own spiritual survival (153) and go directly to heaven (151). On the level of a plumbing-parts manger scene, all this is simple enough, but that is its main shortcoming. It is too simple for the world Skelton finds himself in. In fact, McGuane appears to interpret contemporary life as a combination of ideas from the atomists of ancient Greece and the existentialists of the mid–twentieth century: "But there is a life that is not a life. . . . A silent man wastes his own swerve of molecules; just as a bee 'doing its number on the flower' is as gone to history as if it never was. The thing and its expressions are to be found shaking hands at precisely that point where Neverneverland and Illyria collide with the Book of Revelation under that downpour of grackle droppings that is the present at any given time" (83). Skelton seems to understand that life is both a matter of absurd chance and free will. His swerve of molecules (destiny) could well pass him by because this cosmic meeting of the imagined ("Neverneverland"), the past ("Illyria"), and the future ("Book of Revelation") is a matter of blind chance. Yet if Skelton desires to accomplish more than a spent bee, he must consciously act to effect the future he desires. At least, he must position himself for opportunity should his desired destiny befall him (the swerve connects with the individual). A life of meaning, then, appears to depend somewhat on self-reliance. Like the Sisyphus of Albert Camus, Skelton must accept fate, yet seek to provide his own meaning.

The first step is to go toward that which gives him meaning. His explanation is that guiding is the only thing he can do at all well (93). What he does right is choose to play the game his own way. He finds a trophy fish for Rudleigh, not so much because of the rules of fishing, as because he has courage enough to dare to contradict conventions. He admits finding the fish is blind chance, but the fact remains that he found the fish only because he was willing to go against tradition. He positioned himself and the swerve hit. Conventional expectation had nothing to do with his success.

This boldness runs in Skelton's family; they as a rule go the distance (21). It is also the reason he is attracted to Dance, who is famous as a long-shot artist who experiences success or failure with equal aplomb. And more importantly, this respect for going the distance and playing the long-shot explains why Skelton will not cease until he has either "discovered" or "achieved" a life with meaning. Ultimately, what *Ninety-two in the Shade* asserts is that life exists for those bold enough to attempt to live according to a personally generated philosophy, and what life "means," profound or not, is life itself. If human beings will simply acknowledge it, there is a swerve along every minute. Such a flat statement is not enough for the romantic Skelton; like Payne and Quinn, he is a transcendent Pecos Bill, seeking life in wide-open spaces. He installs a glass bubble atop his dwelling so that he can contemplate the endless sky (142), and the newly built skiff that will take him out on the vast expanse of ocean represents a bold act in his effort to counteract the nothingness of existence (80). Like Payne, Skelton feels that his life, not simply life itself, must have greater meaning than appears possible in contemporary America. He desires a spiritual something, but he is not sure what.

Since he is a romantic (66–67), Skelton can understand the texture of life best when he is confronted with death. Death as an entity possesses the significance necessary to make life precious to the living. It is the clear and present existence of death that makes life "alive" for Skelton. He finds profundity in multiple orgasms, falls in love with the essential human goodness of strangers in restaurants, and overtips a waitress as if to demonstrate that a spark of such goodness resides within himself. Indeed, when he leaves the restaurant someone asks, "Who was that masked man?" (190). Obvious comparison with the Lone Ranger (another incarnation of Pecos Bill) aside, one way not to be a face in the crowd is to put on a mask; Skelton seeks a distinct and romantic identity, if accomplished only in his own imagination and interpreted only by himself.

Through death, then, Skelton discovers his life. To fully treasure one's life is to live secure in the knowledge that one is going to die. Such behavior imbues, as it does for Skelton in his final days, each mundane occurrence with profound meaning. Such meaning is the discovery we can make with Skelton. If life is to be lived, it must be lived as best it can in Hotcakesland, where being alive is the same as having already been to and returned from hell (109). Whether there is an afterlife at all, let alone one with the meaning Skelton seeks, remains a moot point. Like Skelton's father, we cannot know whether our lucky number is "Infinity" or "Waste Disposal" (195).

Goldsboro, Skelton's grandfather, has dealt with life's absurdity in an outlandish way. He got his start in salvage and has been salvaging a more quickened existence from conventional life ever since. Even at age 70, for instance, he will not settle for conventional sex but instead pursues his secretary on a trampoline. Even the ridiculous is preferable to the mundane; a life without an exciting edge to it is not worth living. Goldsboro manages to accomplish his own meaning in life without giving credence to law, organized life's most obvious set of conventions. He too places his own interpretation on the Christian faith. As he reviews his life, he thanks "Christ for the grandiose instinct for creating a vortex that had been his since the turn of the twentieth century" (113). Actually, Goldsboro has created his own existence, made himself the successful crook he is, but when he thanks Christ he demonstrates that he thinks outrageousness is his God-given mandate, his ordained fate. This view makes it unnecessary for him to consider any of the ramifications—ethical or familial—of his actions. There exists only Goldsboro Skelton and the vortex he has made of himself. Unfortunately, even though there is a great whirl of activity and things are drawn to a vortex, a vortex is void at the center. What is missing in the way Goldsboro Skelton deals with the world is warmth, as his relationship with his son and grandson reveals. Even though he defends both to the outside world, he is cold and abrupt when dealing with them personally.

Tom's father is no less committed to a life of outlandishness than the grandfather. If the grandfather parlayed World War I into a personal fortune, the father attempted to achieve the same results from World War II. The father has not been as successful as the grandfather, but he is a more thoughtful man. He is no longer interested in mocking those who live the conventional life (173), and his outlandishness has taken a personal turn; that is, his behavior does not rob from the world at large, but it does dispirit his family. He spends all day in bed with television, his violin, and Shakespeare, and then roams at night in search of drink and sex. In his own way, he attempts to generate meaning in a life he has begun to interpret as meaningless.

Both his father and his grandfather would prefer that Skelton not risk death by guiding, but both men are powerless because of the examples they have set. Both the father and the grandfather have abused the principles of law that keep the republic together. They have sought their own good at the expense of the common good. In their defense, however, they have maintained a sense of humor about life; they seem not to be evil. But they have provided grandson Tom with an undue respect for self-generated codes of behavior, which again, is one of the reasons Dance appeals to him.

Tom admits that it is partly out of respect for Dance that he goes through the life-or-death crisis Dance has engineered (174). Skelton's father knows it is Skelton's respect for lethal romanticism (67) that motivates him, and nothing can be done to stop the sequence of events now in progress. When Skelton asks his father what he would do in the same situation, the father replies that he would go through with it (173). Skelton, then, because of who he is, must carry on this Dance of death. If there are truths in these relationships between sons and fathers, one is that modeled behavior is the only effective teacher, and another is that regardless of Tom's efforts to remain sane (33), craziness in the blood will prevail.

Ironically enough, Dance is bent on his own quest for meaning with the same fierceness but with none of the Skeltonesque finesse. Dance is a strong and blunt Hemingway-code hero extraordinaire. He will not be interfered with, and at the time the novel opens, he has already committed murder. He will not recant. He doesn't want to kill Skelton, a young man he likes and respects, but he has said he would and a man's word is his bond. In the face of death without discipline or glory—which makes such a death distinctly un-Hemingwayesque—such a code is ridiculous; however, Dance remains a sympathetic character because he gives up his life in defense of the only thing that gives his life meaning: his credence (75). People in general and Skelton in particular must take him seriously. For Dance, as well as Skelton, the only option is all or nothing, with nothing tantamount to living life according to someone else's code. Skelton and Dance come together on this issue, each showing the other a kind of love, the love one code hero can have only for another. When the novel ends, Dance and Skelton are side by side, both dead in the same boat, "two foiled and strangely synchronous lives" (197).

They are foils because of their different attitudes toward death. Overwhelmingly self-absorbed, Skelton is fascinated by the possibility of his own death (21, 89). Because he is both religious and romantic, he knows he does not belong in this lunatic nation America has become (54). He wants to live at the bottom of the sea, if not exactly a pair of ragged claws, at least safe from nincompoops (58). Dance, by contrast, is not self-absorbed; he thus thinks of Skelton's death and not his own. Dance is neither religious nor romantic and has no trouble conceding to Skelton a better chance for an eternal reward (161), especially since Dance plans to be alive after the confrontation. If there is any wisdom in this situation, it resides in Dance's remark that one should never kill anybody if it isn't funny (35). Both men violate this dictum—Dance because he cannot tolerate having his credence ignored; Skelton because he takes life too seriously. Skelton maintains that death yields a great cosmic effect when, in reality death is simply the end of all that human beings know of life. While Dance does not think about what life might mean, Skelton thinks too intensely. Since afterlife and significance remain to be seen, the ultimate truth could well be that life is a joke that Tom Skelton cannot take.

The conventional life these characters are so eager not to live is chronicled in the lives of Faron and Jeannie Carter. Carter is a successful fishing guide and a good friend of Dance. Carter is conservative, follows the rules, and always brings in a respectable day's catch. But he never does anything exciting. At the end of the day he is exhausted, and his home life brings him no respite, because Jeannie is obsessed with purchases. She is an example of what can happen if one takes life in the Hotcakesland of commercial America seriously. Everything the Carters own is a showpiece, demonstrating essentially that they are living life as the marketing industry has instructed them to live it. Unfortunately, one of the best guides in Key West cannot pay for all his wife's desires: collection agencies are constantly pursuing them, and Jeannie is constantly purchasing more.

Jeannie's portrait satirizes everything that is lacking in the sort of American woman who never develops her own vision and therefore never demands the reins of her own destiny. Her life is important only when it relates to a man's world. She is a former high school baton twirler whose forte was masturbating her suitors in the backseats of cars. Her life essentially ended when she stopped being the center of adolescent male attention. Now, meaning is available only in purchased items the consumer industry convinces her she cannot live without. She clusters things about herself as if they would ward off death. Even new life is not as important as new acquisitions. Moments after telling Carter that she is finally pregnant, after 20 years, she begins to explain to him the wonders of a self-cleaning oven. McGuane refers to Jeannie the high schooler as "simple pink cake with a slot" (138) and explains that the grown-up Jeannie could replace her obsession for shopping only with group sex behind the high school. The problem with Jeannie is that she is not in control of the way her life is lived. What she represents that the Skeltons do not is that she is as much the victim of commercial America as she is the victimizer of her ever-exhausted, well-meaning husband. Being dictated to by the gods of American consumerism, the text seems to say, is the alternative to trying to live a life of one's own devising, to trying to see a way through the nonsense of life.

Trying to see their way through such nonsense the way the Skeltons do, however, does exact its toll on the women who love them. Even though Miranda claims that sex is the most important thing she has time for (22), she is not simply a sex object for Skelton. In his own perverse way McGuane shows the depth of the Tom-Miranda relationship in the incident in which she has sex with a former lover. Afterward, she wants to share with Skelton the details of her wonderful orgasm. She is not aware of what her ex-lover's orgasm was like; she has not shared her happiness with him; she wants to share it with Tom. Skelton is too jealous to understand, but she tells him he'll have to redefine his sense of innocence, and she will not allow him to besmirch her former sexual relationships. She appears here to be her own person, charting her own course. Ultimately, she agrees that since fidelity is important to Tom, there won't be any more old boyfriends. Her commitment to their relationship is solid. She even becomes involved in a fistfight with Jeannie Carter in Tom's behalf, over the Skelton-Dance feud (160–161).

But ultimately Miranda is subordinated to Skelton's need to guide and his commitment to the macho code he shares—evidently more deeply than he loves her—with Dance. She knows pleading with him will do no good (183), and on the day he dies, she is off the Keys visiting her grandmother, because she cannot face the reality of his impending death. She exists outside the things that matter most to Skelton and is seemingly only an instrument to help heighten the final days of his life with good sex. Were Miranda more clearly self-actualized, she might attempt more strenuous methods than pleading, but she does not. She can only hide her face from the light.

Miranda is essentially a younger version of Skelton's mother. Mrs. Skelton is exhausted from tolerating three generations of Skelton men. Her devotion, unlike Jeannie Carter's, is not to the acquisition of objects but to her men. She is intelligent, is capable of verbal repartee, and receives the respect of all three. But they do not consider her well-being when they decide to live according to their own codes. None of the joys of conventional family life are hers. She decided long ago and continues to decide to do nothing about the outlandishness of their self-reliance.

These women are round characters in that they are capable of emotional exhaustion, can make decisions, can feel in their bones the losses taken by their men. They cannot, however, influence the actions that cause such losses. They are at the mercy of male prerogatives; they are hapless in the face of male fate. In the great plays of life they are on the sidelines, alternately cheering and worrying.

Ultimately, then, in *Ninety-two in the Shade* all the characters have performed their tragic play and found that for them, unlike Rudleigh's fish, there is no benevolent presence to release them after a brave fight. There is evidently only the snickering footman. The novel ends as it begins, with nobody able to understand the trouble Americans are experiencing with their republic. Since there are no solutions, we must, then, remember that perhaps the bravest survival principle is not a "brief soulful howl beside the garbage" (166) but the charting of our own courses on the exciting edge of existence. The effect of moving on the edge is that it not only quickens the moment but also contributes to making the dared and eventual death, even if unquestionably final, a great one.

At the same time, however, daring the great death on the edge of existence may not be what *Ninety-two* means at all. At one point Miranda bakes Tom a cake. Somehow a mouse gets into the oven atop the cake (90–91). It is simply looking for food, doing what comes naturally, doing what it is good at, but it is doing it in the wrong place at the wrong time. When the oven door is opened, the mouse explodes into flames. After very momentary frustration, Miranda cuts off the soiled portion of the cake, and she and Tom, as they had originally planned, each enjoy a piece of what remains. Death may be cosmic, perhaps even explosive, but it does not change the flow or nature of human existence. Tom, Dance, the mouse—none has died for any good reason. Despite Tom Skelton's grace under pressure, his knowing exactly what he wants, and his commitment to live and die for his goal, he discovers that in the wasteland of Hotcakesland America, mice and men die without impact. *Ninety-two in the Shade* remains McGuane's most complex work, literary in its echoes, ambivalent in its resonances.

Chapter Five
Filming the West

Thomas McGuane's four western screenplays (*Rancho DeLuxe, The Missouri Breaks, Tom Horn, Cold Feet*) praise traditional frontier values while at the same time demonstrating that respect for the conventional processes of civilization is the most effective avenue for survival. The lone male protagonists value ultimate possibility through freedom from law until they discover the virtues of modest capitalism and the love of the right woman. The separate protagonists respond to these discoveries idiosyncratically, however, and when the movies are viewed as a tetralogy the larger truth remains that survival is often not possible if the protagonists are to remain faithful to their natures. In essence, McGuane depicts the West's inability to fulfill its own frontier myths.

In all four films most of the outlaws and ranchers who live firmly in the belief of ultimate possibility fail to survive: self-fulfillment through outlawry is as impossible as big ranching. Large ranchers risk destruction through their own ambition, and outlaws learn that the only way to survive in the West is to follow the ordinary dictates of civilization. The conclusion of *Cold Feet,* however, moves these ideas slightly off center, seemingly demonstrating that law bending in the service of the good is possible in the contemporary West.

Of Rustlers and Indians

Even though *Rancho DeLuxe*[1] is set in and around contemporary Livingston, Montana, the young protagonists, Jack and Cecil, live by rustling. They seek to undermine the established order by such frontier behavior. Basically, they are living in a romantic West that does not exist and probably never did. At first they shoot and butcher with a chain saw only the occasional steer or sheep. They don't want to become rich and infamous; they simply want to meet expenses. They pay their rent, for instance, with fresh meat, still warm.

McGuane's concern with the oppressiveness of contemporary conventional existence is apparent in at least two sequences. At one point Jack flies home to visit his parents, upwardly mobile suburbanites somewhere in the East. This is his first visit home since his divorce, and he will not be back. Unbeknownst to Jack, his parents invite Anna, his ex-wife, for dinner. Jack demonstrates no respect for his parents, peevishly questioning their "goddam judgment." When Anna protests that she still loves him, he replies, "I don't care." He explains to her that being single is the only way he can live and that they cannot re-form their marriage, because they "make each other insane" and "mutilate each other." He admits he does love her but exclaims, "I just want to be rid of it." Then, flying into a rage, he destroys his parents' expensive furniture and fine china. He simply cannot function in this cleaned and polished environment.

The other sequence concerns Jack and Cecil's relationship with Betty and Mary Fargo, two local young women. Mary, still in high school, is consumed by a concern for cosmic consciousness and the *I ching*. Betty works in a local fly-tying factory, and if her sister can be believed, engages in sexual sport with every manner of Livingston male. They make an energetic foursome, frolicking and doping in the Crazy Mountains. McGuane is careful that we understand the foursome is not to be confused with conventional and conforming adults. Jack and Cecil refer to Mary and Betty as "the girls," and Mary and Betty, burlesquing conventional code words, refer to Jack and Cecil, whose existences they are quickening with frequent and intense sexual coupling, as "nice boys."

At one point they are all four in the same bed in Jack and Cecil's house when the girls' father, Wilbur, breaks in on them. Wilbur, a member of Livingston's established social order, is in truth more worried about recovering his Lincoln Continental Mark IV; every time he mentions the car, he gives its full name. Then in a supremely McGuanesque comic scene, he calls in all the neighbors and relatives to "see the floozies and the whoremongers." All appear in doorways and windows, and he tells them to "see what the world has come to." He explains to Jack and Cecil that he is slow to tolerate "filth and evil," and Jack retaliates by shooting at him with a handgun. Then Jack orders Wilbur to go down on his knees and apologize to his daughters. When Wilbur does so, Jack says, "If you had any right to come in here and do this, you wouldn't be such a coward and fall down on your knees at my command." The value system from which Wilbur is operating does not apply. It is the value system of inherited conformity. If it were a value system into which Wilbur had profoundly invested his own intelligence and understanding, he would not have been so quick to wilt at Jack's command. If he exhibited self-generated integrity, he would have remained true to a self-established code.

The rustlers then demonstrate their lack of respect for Wilbur's pride of ownership by taking the Lincoln up into the mountains and shooting it full of holes with a Sharps buffalo rifle.[2] (That they own this old-time piece illustrates the boys' romantic link with the past. At one point they refer to themselves as "about the last of the plainsmen.") Like Jack when he broke up his parents' dining room, these two "plainsmen," in ruining the car, are exploding the civilized order. For Wilbur the car symbolizes achievement, indicates his place in the social strata, and commands respect from his own kind. But the protagonists will not respect such achievement.

McGuane's sense of outlawry is further clarified by the rustlers' confrontation with John Brown, the most successful rancher in the territory. Loud and blustery, Brown is McGuane's personification of the new West. His pedigree is inauthentic. He does not derive from a long line of Montana ranchers but is instead a successful beauty-parlor operator from Schenectady, New York. He has built his empire not with tradition or skill but with Eastern money and is proud of his success in the West: "We raise very correct cattle here." The boys' penny-ante rustling annoys Brown: "At this point in the twentieth century I'm not going to be plagued by rustlers." And more seriously, Brown is bored and impatient because there are no more ranches to absorb into his expanding empire. Tired of having him pout about the house, Cora, his wife, suggests he hold a press conference and declare war on the rustlers.

Jack and Cecil are up to the challenge. They steal Brown's prize seedbull, Baseheart of Bozeman Canyon, and hold him for a ransom of $50,000. Brown regards the "animal as [his] signature on the American West" and expediently pays off. That the bull is named Baseheart is a further comment on Brown's profane exploitation of the contemporary West. He has westered not so much to seek fulfillment as to dominate. McGuane comments further on the failure of frontier spirit in the contemporary West when he has the protagonists abandon the bull in a room at a Holiday Inn, a glaring example of uniformity. With an out-of-focus television flickering in the background, Baseheart simply walks about the room destroying everything and leaving modernity in a shambles. The modern West, we can believe, is no place for an animal as strong and as natural as a bull.

McGuane is careful to demonstrate that Jack and Cecil, while outlaws, are not bad men. Even though they can't think of ways to spend the ransom money, they decide next to steal a truckload of "living veal." They steal not for money but "just to keep from falling asleep." Rustling is a way to stave off the boredom and routine of ordinary existence; indeed, as they go about their rustling, they mention how awake they are. Rustling is also another way of linking themselves to the romantic West of the past. And as romantics, they do not steal from Brown out of spite. In their own way, they appreciate him and give him his due: "Brown is not so bad either. He keeps some of these shitass tourists from putting aluminum house trailers on a quarter acre of pasture." They are, as they claim, "sportsmen."

This aspect of sportsmanship surfaces again at the film's conclusion. Brown hires Henry Beige, "a two thousand year-old rangeland cornball" and stock detective, to put a stop to the rustling. Before becoming a stock detective, Beige had been a horse thief, "the very best"—he could disseminate stolen horses into a four-state area in 48 hours. But he was apprehended and spent World War II breaking horses at Rancho DeLuxe, the Montana prison ranch. He decided to reform not because he thought horse thievery was morally wrong but because he understood that his outlawry cost him all the fun of the war. After Beige catches Jack and Cecil, he tells Brown he doesn't care whether he receives his fee, because he's "in it for the sport."

The difference between Beige's West and Brown's West is, as their names imply, one of shading. Brown is somewhat too solid, a degree too inflexible, a little too formidable to be admired. Beige, on the other hand, is lighter in tone. He doesn't take himself quite so seriously; he is not as definite in his approach to life. While Brown jolts about the countryside tracking down leads and sending bullets off to the crime lab, Beige dreams in the bunkhouse and pretends to be a broken-down has-been under his "niece" Laura's care. Lulled off guard by what he thinks is Laura's love for him, Curt, one of the ranch hands in league with Jack and Cecil, confides in Laura and the protagonists are caught red-handed.

The capture is a fine piece of comedy. All the surrounding population stage a potluck dinner at the mouth of the road the boys will have to employ to escape with the living veal. Between pieces of peach pie, Beige mounts his horse, and in the manner of the romantic West, rides up and orders the boys out of the truck at gunpoint. The apprehension brings applause from the populace, who have watched the dramatic capture from lawn chairs. Real westerners, perhaps especially the ones who now ride the range in lawn chairs, McGuane seems to be saying, prefer the romantic version.

When Brown belatedly appears and exclaims that he's determined the identity of the rustlers, Beige explains that modern methods "just don't get it done. When you're dealing with people, you've got to be human." He presents Brown with his bill and tells him he can use it to "wipe the pablum off your chin." In the West Brown is a mere infant. His is not the true way of those who are in it for the sport. Brown is taking his place in the West much too seriously. Being the best and the biggest is not as important as playing the game. Finally, it is Jack and Cecil who achieve the frontier life. When we last see them, they are wranglers at Rancho DeLuxe, where they spend all day on horseback on the open range chasing cows. They have become real cowboys. For recreation, they walk coins between their fingers and practice simpleminded card tricks, traditional prison pastimes. The closing music of the film points up the truth of the situation. As the credits roll, Jimmy Buffet, McGuane's brother-in-law, sings:

> The game is done
> Nobody lost and nobody won
> Shuffle the cards and play it again
> It really doesn't matter
> If we lose we still win.

As Jack says, he and Cecil "will find a way" to get along. The "way" McGuane's protagonists are seeking is a delivery from ordinariness. If they are required to create a nineteenth-century West to ensure their own success, they will.

An interesting sidelight to *Rancho DeLuxe* is that the film exists in a separate television version, available regularly on the late show. The earthy language has been silenced, and the raucous fornication scenes have been eliminated. In their place, presumably for reasons of running time, appear scenes not used in the theatrical version. The new footage demonstrates that McGuane possesses more insight into the lives of contemporary Indians in Montana than his readers might heretofore have supposed.

In the theatrical version, Cecil and his ancestors are generally played for humor. When Jack tells Cecil he has secured a date for him with Betty's sister Mary, Cecil responds, "Shall I bring a lot of rubbers?" The remark in and of itself can be construed as normal for a young man on the prowl, but Jack finds it to be singularly ethnic: "Indians, Jesus."

At another point, Cecil in mock solemnity tells Jack, "Before you whites came here, we had a simple existence in these Cheyenne Mountains under this big sky." Again Jack gets the final and white word: "Your relatives were primarily honky tie hounds from Iowa and buck-toothed squaw humpers from the East." His comment simply denies Cecil any hope of an ancestry he can be proud of. Jack's remark makes particularly empty a later speech by Cecil's father, who talks of European royalty existing somewhere in the bloodline. In this scene Cecil and his father are fishing, and in response to his father's comment that the "old boys on the reservation" used to eat grasshoppers, Cecil, displaying a contented smile, munches one. Indians, it seems, are given to both misconceptions of self-identity and simple silliness.

The restored scenes, however, depict Indians in a more complex light. In one, Cecil arrives home to find his father asleep in front of a television flashing images of wild, screaming Indians. The contrast is clear: McGuane's Indians are not the conventional Hollywood version. Once the television is turned off, Cecil's father tells the story of Bob Not-a-Small-Crow, a Northern Cheyenne who passed as a Cree to secure a propane franchise. The man now lives in Los Angeles and owns a pancake restaurant; Cecil's father has just seen him on a quiz show.

Seeing the man reminds Cecil's father of the death of his own father. The old man died when they were snowed in without a vehicle in the Missouri breaks. Cecil's father had to strap his father to spruce planks and guide him out like a toboggan. He left him in Bob Not-a-Small-Crow's propane storage for nine days until the blizzard stopped. Then Not-a-Small-Crow helped him transport the old man to the Indian burial grounds. What both Cecil and his father wonder about is whether Not-a-Small-Crow tells the story to customers in his pancake house. We also learn that the Cheyenne now calls himself Bob Small and that Cecil's father is unemployed.

From this touching scene between father and son, we understand that Indians have always lived a rather elemental existence and that survival within and without the Indian community can well depend on the denial of one's own identity. Their one hope lies with the oral tradition. Only in the telling of stories can the truth of their human existence be maintained. Only among themselves are they allowed to speak of the past with dignity.

Cecil and his father also speak of John Brown's acquisitive tendencies and feel pity for a man who is "trying to be King." The truth that some people are so busy trying to rule that they forget to live is an old one perhaps, but when played off against the simple loving relationship of Cecil and his father, John Brown's boisterous and self-important role in the contemporary West appears empty indeed.

McGuane later employs this Indian sense of profound yet simple truth more boldly in his novel *Nobody's Angel*. Patrick Fitzpatrick and David Catches, a Northern Cheyenne, come together to revenge themselves on each other for the death of Mary Fitzpatrick, Patrick's sister and David's lover. That Indian people are not highly regarded by the white community is quickly made clear when Patrick's grandfather explains David's primary shortcoming: "He'd try to tell you how it was."[3] The young Indian appears not to understand that only the whites know what the truth is. The grandfather, however, goes on to admit that he began to sense David might actually interpret the events of life in ways whites cannot and that David would "give you the feeling he'd know where Mary had gone." (124).

Even though Patrick fortifies himself with whiskey—his only means of survival at the moment—he has no white defense against simple Indian truth. Despite Patrick's assertion that Indians know that nothing matters, David will not share his romantic nihilism, will not confirm Patrick's notion that "there isn't any use" (135). In the end Patrick admits that Mary meant more to David than she did to him. Patrick has no defense for the simple fact that David loved Mary, that she died because she was insane, not because David let her die.

One cannot, McGuane contends, write about Montana without developing a strong sense of Indians. "From the inside out I really don't know anything about Indian culture, but we can't walk from the house a minute and a half before we'll hit tipi rings. This ranch was part of the old Crow reservation. We have Indian graves all around. They really were here. It is the deeper human echo of this country and you should feel it in your writing."

Of Rustlers and Ranchers

The next two screenplays tone down the glamour of the frontier motif without conceding anything to the world of civilized achievement. In *Missouri Breaks*,[4] Tom Logan is a member of a band of men who rustle horses from Montana ranchers. The largest, most successful rancher in the area is David Braxton, who "acts like God" and typifies the big men who settled the West. He "was in the California gold fields before he was eighteen," and Montana is his "fourth frontier." We recognize him immediately as a profane man; nothing, not even the desires of his family, will stand in the way of his success. Rustlers have taken 7 percent of his stock the previous season, and when he catches a member of Logan's band, he hangs him.

Logan's men bemoan the new West. Whereas formerly a captured rustler would receive only a few months in prison, now there's "something new in the air": the advance of a civilization that makes rich men richer. Even though Braxton understands that the thieves have "a million good reasons for being on hard times," he asserts they must be obliterated or they will "waste everything." He is not one to surrender 7 percent of his stock to the downtrodden. To this end he hires Lee Clayton, a stock detective, or regulator. The popular term for such men is *drygulcher,* one who "shoots people and don't ever get near em." Clayton's job is to simply, not fairly, eliminate undesirable elements. We understand that Braxton's method of civilizing is not above savagery in the name of decency.

Outlawry may be a dying art, but Braxton's way of life offers no fulfilling alternative. He prides himself on his own rational prowess and on the
3,500 volumes of English literature in his library, but his frontier home is
missing the major civilizing ingredient—the influence of a woman. His
daughter Jane is a strong-minded young woman who doesn't approve of her
father's methods. She wants to "talk about the wild West and how to get
the hell out of it." Her mother left Braxton after three years of marriage:
"She listened very carefully to [Braxton,] . . . weighed every word, and then
she up and ran off with the first unreasonable man she could find." When
Lee Clayton asks Braxton, "Why is it you mental wizards can never keep
your women?" the rancher loses himself and begins to rant. Armed with
nothing but his own profane sense of achievement, he has no self-
controlling resolve at the center of his character.

This failure of feminine partnership is illustrated in another scene. After
rustling all of Braxton's stock, the outlaws split up to sell them a few head
at a time. One of the rustlers is staying overnight with a family to whom he
has just sold three head. At the supper table, the rancher, obviously proud
of his intellectual capabilities, pontificates that Thomas Jefferson said he
was a warrior so that his son could be a farmer so that *his* son could be a
poet. The rancher further explains that he raises cattle so that his son can become a merchant and his grandson can move to the East Coast and "own a
sailboat." The rancher demonstrates the same notion of civilizing the frontier that Braxton does: one exploits the frontier to serve capitalistic upward
mobility, not simply to provide for one's family. When the rancher's wife is
ushering the rustler to the bunkhouse, she backs up against the wall and has
standing sex with him. The act seems unmotivated; they have hardly spo-
ken. Two interpretations immediately present themselves: (a) she is simply
tired of her mental wizard of a husband, or (b) worse yet, her husband has
included her favors as partial payment for the horses. The latter explanation
seems stronger, because she is very businesslike. She tells the rustler he has
only five minutes, and she refuses to step all the way out of her "drawers."
With either interpretation, McGuane's ranchers are decidedly pragmatic
men who see no romance on the frontier.

The rustlers buy a small ranch near Braxton so that they can more easily
relay the stolen stock out of the country. All the rustlers except Tom Logan
take a negative view of ranch life. Logan says that his folks always wanted a
place "and they was good people," and so he doesn't think there is anything
wrong with a ranch as such. Unlike the other outlaws, he is respectful of
such ties to his family. (Cal, one of the other outlaws, brags of robbing and
almost murdering the uncle who raised him, for instance.) Still, Logan is se-

verely unhappy when the band decides to venture into Canada to steal horses and leaves him with the responsibility of tending the ranch. He may not mind the ranch, but he does mind missing the excitement of the trip. Left behind, Logan cleans up the orchard, plants a garden, and develops an ingenious irrigating system. Despite his continuous protestations that ranch life is too dull for him, he begins to take pride in his work. Even though the ranch in actuality means nothing to the outlaws' plans, Logan begins to organize it. During this time, he and Jane Braxton fall in love, a complication that bothers Braxton because his daughter's leaving him would require him to acknowledge that his household is cold and cruel and doesn't deserve a woman at its hearth. Logan, a desperate man at odds with society, appears in Jane Braxton's eyes to be a better man than her father. Logan presents the possibility of a relationship more fulfilling than that of her father and mother.

As the story concludes, Lee Clayton has murdered all the rustlers except Logan. He thinks Logan has been burned up in a cabin fire, and so he is off his guard. Thus Logan is able to sneak up on him while he sleeps and cut his throat. Clayton represents the savagery required to settle the frontier, a savagery that takes all the enjoyment out of the West. As one Braxton hand put it, "It wasn't near as gloomy around here when we only had just rustlers." Without warning and at a safe distance, Clayton eliminated all of Logan's band: he drowned one at the end of a rope, burned out and then spiked another, shot one during sex, and shot another while the man sat in an outhouse. The eradication of Lee Clayton is more important than the elimination of rustling, because he personifies the vicious, profane, any-means-to-an-end methods of progress.

The final scenes of the movie present a small problem: they are not of McGuane's authorship. They are instead the work of the renowned Hollywood script doctor Robert Towne. In the screen version, Braxton meets his end for possessing the same viciousness as Clayton. Out of patience with her father's views, Jane decides to leave the ranch, and Braxton disintegrates. As the film ends, Braxton is entirely without substance. He is bibbed like a baby, and his butler is feeding him mashed eggs, most of which run down the once godlike rancher's chin. Logan arrives intent on killing Braxton for hiring Clayton; however, after witnessing the sad state of the defeated land baron, he recants. But Braxton fires the first shot, and Logan kills him. The views personified by Braxton and Clayton are hollow. Achievement for achievement's sake and the unquestioned respect for bigness are the ideas of pragmatic men without hearts, of men who—because they are not fully de-

veloped human beings—still have pablum on their chins. No full realization of life will be possible so long as the heartless hold sway.

In the final scene Jane Braxton calls on Tom as he is preparing to leave
the relay ranch for good. She too is planning to leave and tells him, "I don't
want to spend the rest of my life trying to get back at somebody." She is announcing here that she is not going to enact the code of the frontier that requires revenge for the killing of a friend or relative. There has been enough
killing. She never believed in her father's ways, and she is not going to sub-
scribe to them now. She then asks Logan where he'll be "in about six
months." He replies, "North of the breaks. There's the Little Rockies up
there and a lot of little valleys supposed to have water year round." Jane's
final facial expression leads us to believe she'll be there, too. The message is
that one can be happy in the "little" rockies and the "little" valleys. Life—
thanks to year-round water—is possible without the bigness Braxton
sought. If outlaw Tom Logan is to survive, it will be on such a little place,
not an expansive spread. If he is to be fulfilled, it will be because Jane
Braxton will be there as well.

McGuane's own ending exists in the published version of *The Missouri
Breaks.* McGuane confirms that this ending is indeed his and explains that
the film version in which Logan shoots Braxton is Towne's execution of star
Jack Nicholson's wishes. Adds McGuane, "I thought they were silly ideas
and wouldn't do them."[5]

The thematic concerns of the published ending appear in one compact
final scene. As Logan enters the house, Braxton is alone in the library. He is
not insane but simply "frightened and unshaven."[6] Braxton claims that he
lost control of Clayton, and Logan replies, "I don't think you did," meaning
that he thinks Clayton followed orders exactly as Braxton directed. But in
this version, revenge on Braxton is not Logan's concern; he goes immediately to Jane in the upstairs hallway. Jane asks him, "Are your friends dead?"
and when he does not respond, adds, "Were they all you had?" Logan answers, "Just about" (122–23), and we understand he has been stripped of
his old outlaw life and is ready to begin a new and more conventional life
with Jane. He then leads Jane into her father's bedroom and closes the door.
Despite the scene's macho-sexual overtones (Are we to believe, for instance,
that Logan's sexual ardor has not been dampened by the killing of his
friends and his own killing of Clayton?), the symbolism is easily read: the
profane Braxton has been replaced in his own house by Logan, a man with
less capitalistic success but more human potential.

The final shot of the published screenplay establishes the defeat of
Braxton's way of life: "Braxton stands in cold morning light staring toward

the open front door" (123). Logan has shown Braxton the door. While this ending is less exciting than a shoot-out, Braxton is symbolically just as dead; he is as cold as the morning light.

Of Outlaws and Cattlemen

The problem of authorship also exists with *Tom Horn.*[7] McGuane has first screenplay credit here but shares billing with the veteran writer Bud Shrake. Shrake explains that McGuane's original script was 220 pages, much too long for a screenplay; the normal length is around 120 pages. For Shrake, "It was like they gave me a 747 and told me to turn it into a sports-car."[8] Shrake dropped the first 100 pages, which concerned Horn's Indian scouting days, his capturing of Geronimo, and his subsequent fall into per-petual drunkenness. Then he cut and refined the last 120 pages, leaving the script "basically McGuane's." The problem was that McGuane's "beauti-fully constructed scenes" often ran to as many as 20 pages and would have resulted in a movie that was too slowly paced. Shrake explains that he couldn't simply throw out pages but had to work the scenes down to a film-able 3 or 4. Of the scenes cited here, McGuane says those depicting the cattlemen's association "are me, but only more or less."[9] Shrake says the thrust of the scenes is McGuane's, but the distinction between which words belong to which author is blurred. McGuane says the flashbacks "are not me," but Shrake explains that the scenes as originally written are not flash-backs but come earlier in the script. Shrake says he shortened the dialogue but adds that Glendolene's words "are definitely [McGuane's] speeches." Shrake maintains that star Steve McQueen loved McGuane and McGuane's work and "had somebody told him it was all right to film a movie that cost forty million dollars and took four hours to show, he would have done it." It is easy to see from this brief discussion that without question, movies are art by committee, and to readily agree with McGuane when he says, "The movies aren't much of a place to view a writer's thoughts, I'm afraid."

The conflicts between the outlaw life and civilizing society are also central to *Tom Horn,* based somewhat but not always accurately on the incidents leading to the hanging of the famous drygulcher in 1903. Horn is em-ployed by a Wyoming cattlemen's association to put an end to rustling, and he methodically goes about his business with a high-powered rifle. During the process he is attracted to Glendolene Kimmel, a local schoolteacher, and for a brief time courts her.

The film demonstrates that the conventional life requires a deromanti-cized West. The members of the cattlemen's association are not to be respected. John Colville, a positive force in the story, refers to their settlement as a "two-bit town" and characterizes the exact worth of their lives negatively: "Here in Jerkville where the yokels is busy flicking dandruff off their mail-order suits, they forget that it was men like [Tom Horn] that made it safe and possible for 'em to lead out their dull little lives." And the ranchers demonstrate the conventional concern for appearances. They hire Horn, telling him he has a free hand to either kill rustlers or bring them in for trial, whichever he sees fit. Horn, a man of violence who has lived his life entirely on lawless frontiers, chooses the former and litters the new West with bodies. The association becomes alarmed because people know Horn is working for them and they are afraid of "having [their] names splattered all over the newspapers." That killing is a crime against humanity doesn't bother them; what troubles them is that they will be caught in an "embarrassing situation." Horn is eventually brought to trial for killing a teenager and is convicted because of an ambitious prosecuting attorney who "needs to hang [him] to get elected" to political office. The motivations of the greater and conventional society are ignobly self-serving and predicated on fear.

At the same time that it is critical of the cattlemen, the film is critical of outlawry. Horn fails to survive because he is not amenable to the fulfilling forces of Glendolene Kimmel. She personifies a view of life entirely outside Horn's ken. She's "had a romance with the West since she was old enough to read," and because she's lived in a number of locations she sees herself as "an adventuress." This term confuses Horn, who thinks an adventuress is "a girl that worked in dance halls." But Glendolene counters that an adventuress is "a girl who goes on adventures." She even indicates that her relationship with Horn could be an adventure. This is a new note for a McGuane film. Being a female schoolteacher, a stereotypically staid profession, can be an adventure. And even something as conventional as a love affair can be an adventure. The message here is that aspects of the conventional life need not be seen as dull and boring. One need not live outside ordinary society to attain fulfillment. And besides, outlaw adventuring can be purposelessly dangerous. At one point Horn and Glendolene are engaging in a romantic interlude. She is relaxing in a cattle watering tank, and they are speaking of love. Suddenly a gunman rides in at full gallop, firing at Horn. Horn shoots him out of the saddle and then clubs him to death. The scene ends on a close-up of Glendolene with the gunman's blood all over her face and shoulders, as if to say that this man of violence has dirtied her romantic notion of life in the West.

Before the gunman rides up, Glendolene asks Horn if he cares for her. He doesn't answer her question but points out that even though he cares for his horse, he has "never even given it a name." The kind of relationship that Glendolene seeks is foreign to Horn. Not only can he not commit himself to her, he does not understand what she needs from him. The last time we see her, she and Horn are breaking up. She tells him, "You're a bad man and I know it. And if I let you talk me out of it, I'll be lost forever. And my adventures in this life won't mean anything because you'll have seduced my soul and drawn me into your world."

Outlawry, then, while it appears to offer more excitement than the ordinary life, does not provide fulfillment in and of itself. Unlike Tom Logan, Horn cannot be drawn out of his outlaw life by the fulfilling forces of a woman, and thus perishes. McGuane appears to believe that the romantic myth permeates and motivates life in the American West but exists only as myth. The West is actually no different from any other former frontier where civilization has overtaken possibility and established conformity.

Of Outlaws and Horses

Cold Feet,[10] set in the contemporary West, continues McGuane's investigation into the possibilities of the outlaw life. The script was originally written as a collaboration with Jim Harrison in 1976. Harrison wrote the original and third drafts, McGuane the second. In 1987, when producers became interested in the project, Harrison was unavailable, and so McGuane handled preproduction conferences with director Robert Dornhelm by himself and gave the story a massive reorganization, eliminating, among other things, the original main character. The movie centers on three third-rate outlaws—Monte Latham, a dopey fun-lover; Kenny Pruitt, a soldier-of-fortune psychopath; and Maureen Linoleum, a nymphomaniac with an equal passion for food. The three smuggle Mexican emeralds into the United States after embedding them surgically in the abdomen of a great stallion, Infidel.

After a double cross, Monte brings the stallion to his brother Buck's ranch in Blue Duck, Montana. The plot thickens when Buck and his wife Laura see the stallion as a means to the financial security necessary to save the ranch. They promptly line up their 41 brood mares to await Infidel's expertise. Monte's 12-year-old daughter Rosemary also arrives at the ranch—directly from survival school in Colorado—closely followed by the angry Kenny and Maureen.

As in McGuane's early novels, black humor appears throughout when least expected. Just as he is about to be murdered, the veterinarian who embeds the emeralds promises not to "breathe a word." Monte tours the ranch in a golf cart. Kenny, mostly a legend in his own mind, explains the difference between passionate and cold killing: "Don't get mad, turn pro." Maureen, in bed with a stranger, begins blowing on the man's duck call. After Buck kills Kenny, he remarks, "I just hate out-of-staters."

Two elements make this script distinctly different from the three earlier McGuane films: Infidel and Rosemary. The stallion illustrates the sacred feeling McGuane has developed for horses. From the beginning Monte distinguishes himself from the other outlaws because of his discomfort at killing the horse simply to get the emeralds out of hiding. In his crooked head there resides a faint notion that there may be an element to life more important than greed. The horse represents a spiritual sacredness Monte seems not to find anywhere else, an idea reinforced when Rosemary falls in love with the horse. Through the horse Monte becomes reacquainted with his daughter and his responsibility to become the father she thinks he is. Thus, horse and child serve as avenues for Monte, the script's most likable character, to approach redemption. The ranch itself serves the same purpose. It is the old family place; both Monte and Buck were raised there. It represents family, roots—a spiritual reality larger than simply a place to hide out. It draws Monte back; the stallion is his contribution to maintaining their collective past and insuring their future.

Buck and Laura present a note of ambiguity. Ostensibly, they are the contented conventional couple, living happily among their flowers and horses. They seem to represent all that is good; indeed, they are the guardians of Rosemary as the story ends. But they are not as truehearted as they appear. When Monte first arrives with the horse, they sense something is amiss, but they give way to their need to survive. They must find some way to keep from losing the ranch: "We'd owe it all to Monte, the crook. Wouldn't that be funny?" Dishonesty in the service of the good evidently becomes more noble than simple dishonesty.

In the same way, Buck, the hardworking, "weathered" cowboy, shoots less than straight in the film's denouement. First, he puts Kenny off guard, achieving the villain's trust by lying to him and then kills him from behind by kicking him into a vat of boiling horses that are dog-food bound. He next lies to the sheriff, telling him that Kenny has escaped with Infidel. As the final credits roll, Buck ushers Infidel back to the ranch ready to stand stud and secure a home for the conventional family unit. Good guys have been outwitting bad guys since western movies began, of course—and bad guys deserve it—but good guys have not been getting away with lying to honest sheriffs in order to maintain the sanctity of the hearth.

Buck and Laura, in their defense, do not know that the horse is carrying emeralds—which establishes the final symbol that the horse himself is a jewel. They are acting solely in the interest of maintaining frontier myths of family survival. In this way, *Cold Feet* is a quietly more mature film than the earlier three. Buck and Laura are not flat characters like Brown, Braxton, or the Wyoming Cattlemen's Association. Neither is Buck clearly a horse thief in the old sense; he is, however, undergoing hard times and, like the westerners of the nineteenth century, ready to exploit whatever frontier opportunities lie in his path. The West of the late twentieth century demands, it seems, outlawry from those who wish to maintain the inviolability of the home. McGuane's cinematic West, then, remains a nineteenth-century West, if not in possibility then at least in spirit.

Chapter Six
Panama: Personalizing the Republic

Overview

Thomas McGuane sees *Ninety-two in the Shade* as signaling the end of his career as a strictly comic novelist. The change came about because he grew older, experiencing the deaths of his sister and father and enduring the censure of the press for his seemingly unstable public behavior. The result was that his vision developed greater depth: "I felt that to go on writing with as much flash as I had tried previously was to betray some of the serious things I had been trying to say. . . . The most drastic attempt [to work out this conflict] was in *Panama*, which I wrote in the first person in this sort of blazing confessional style. In terms of feeling my shoulder to the wheel and my mouth to the reader's ear, I have never been so satisfied as I was when I was writing that book."[1] Unfortunately, even though with *Panama* McGuane received some of his most positive reviews, a larger number of reviewers panned the book as a self-serving effort far below the promise of earlier novels. That *Panama* should occasion such a vitriolic response still baffles McGuane: "I thought that this cataclysmic howl of despair was still essentially comic. I saw it as comedy stretched to the snapping point. I guess most people just felt it had snapped."

McGuane's concern for the conflicts between the protagonist and the prevailing attitudes of his times continues in *Panama*. Chester Hunnicutt Pomeroy has become an overnight sensation by publicly personifying the debasement possible on the dark side of the human imagination; he has experienced "all the nightmares, all the loathsome, toppling states of mind, all the evil things that go on behind closed eyes."[2] He has, for instance, emerged from the anus of a frozen elephant to duel with a baseball-batting-practice machine. He has also brought an end to his career by vomiting on the mayor of New York.

As the novel opens, Chester has returned to Key West in hope of re-creating a stable life. His major hope is that he can reconcile with his wife, Catherine, who remained loyal until he became "a real animal and a national disgrace" (47). They were married in Panama, and that seems to be the only place their relationship actually worked. Even though she still loves him, Catherine wants nothing to do with him. His behavior is still too bizarre for her. At one point he nails his hand to Catherine's door, and at another, snorts cocaine off the sidewalk. To compound his problems, he has lost his memory and given up all hope for a meaningful life. When Catherine does show signs of wanting to return, Chester desires to reform for her, but such an effort at stability is beyond him. The debilitating crassness he finds in commercial America requires that he respond with outlandish behavior. Catherine wants a conventional happy marriage as the main goal; Chester wants to be illustrious (123). When she realizes Chester will never change, she leaves him forever to "the emptiness [he] call[s] home" (79).

Critical Reception

Panama, McGuane's first novel after five years of highly sensationalized film-colony behavior, received sharp criticism. Influential and negative reviews appeared in the *New York Times Book Review, Time,* and the *New Republic.* The general tone was that McGuane had not written up to his gifts, was not fulfilling the potential greatness signaled by the first three novels. The *Time* notice is a scant and unsigned, but biting, three paragraphs. We are reminded that McGuane was on his way to becoming "A Major American Writer,"[3] the Hemingway of the drug generation. Celebrity, both McGuane's and the protagonist's, is the villain. The novel is tired, the protagonist and the American culture exhausted, but the despair is unearned. Pomeroy is too narcissistic to be interesting and the novel too smug.

In the *Times Book Review,* Richard Elman sees the work not at all as a novel but as a movie he thinks he's already seen. In fact, he finds *Panama* so unimpressive that he has trouble remembering plot details. He finds the dialogue uninspiring and thinks the antics McGuane intends to be a reflection of the sick culture are really nothing more than ordinary behavior. Elman is tired of the exhausted. He concludes that such stories go better in the movies, where "everybody would say that those casual sliding shots and lackadaisical bits of dialogue were art."[4] While the review of *Ninety-two in the Shade* appeared on page 1, Elman's piece appears on page 36, buried with the notes on contributors.

In the *New Republic,* Donald R. Katz perceptively analyzes the McGuane oeuvre before focusing on *Panama.* Katz thinks that the early McGuane novels accurately charted the nation's course in the late sixties and early seventies, and asserts, perhaps jokingly, that they were welcomed with the same joy one evidences on discovering new drugs. The McGuane protagonist is motivated by the old virtues, "culled bits of frontier ethic and inviolate wilderness verities that used to define American manhood."[5] McGuane heroes are slightly "mind-mangled" young white men who suffer Faulknerian and Hemingwayesque angst but have no place to come to manhood in Hotcakesland society. "All they can hope for," says Katz, "is enough disdain to rise above it, and all they can do is howl or die" (38). McGuane portrays lunacy romanticized to a point that is almost worth the pain, because it is healthier for one's soul to succumb to the manic maintenance of one's own code than to capitulate to the crass expectations of middle-class life.

Katz, however, finds *Panama* a lesser and bitter book about an alternative American dream that never came to pass. The novel is without moving characters, strong prose, or real pain. While McGuane is easily the best writer of stories about brilliant and sensitive young aristocrats since the 1920s (an implied evocation of Fitzgerald), his work continues to fall short of greatness. He is not, for example, Tolstoy or Dostoyevski. Katz asserts that McGuane is preoccupied with "cunt and death," whereas the Russians write of "love and immortality" (39). Katz concludes by implying that greater truths would be available were McGuane's protagonists to dig more deeply into the wreckage of their times. Suffering, it seems, could be more deeply depicted than as simple insanity.

Gary Fisketjon in the *Village Voice,* on the contrary, credits McGuane with the discovery of new and deeper insights. The author, Fisketjon claims, has moved on from "smartass-at-large" to a maturing writer of "uncompromised honesty."[6] What McGuane is honest about is the individual's participation in and contribution to the collective ugliness of America. While not calling the book autobiography, Fisketjon praises McGuane for taking the risk of exposing himself. The novel is more personal, more empathic, and less disdainful, the author sifting through the wreckage of his life, searching for what he has lost because of his celebrity. In mirroring the protagonist's pain, Fisketjon asserts, McGuane has taken up a task more difficult than satire; he has sought to balance suffering and understanding.

In the *New Yorker,* Susan Lardner notes McGuane's career as a screenwriter and director and conjectures that because of his Hollywood experience, he has begun to see life as a circus performance and become apprehensive about fame. Lardner, like Fisketjon, does not find the author writing beneath his gifts; rather, she applauds his first work composed in the first person and concludes her review "hungry for more."[7] She does, however, make some interesting if undeveloped assertions about McGuane's women. She notes that no McGuane male has ever met his match with a McGuane female. Lardner sees Catherine as a "Penelopean whore at her idealized best" (154) but finds Mercelline, Catherine's bisexual friend, a welcome relief from Chester Pomeroy's self-absorption.

A Reading

Ultimately, *Panama* is a more complex novel than the reviewers indicate. McGuane again focuses on commercial American culture, on the malaise of the age, but his protagonist here does not so much rage against the age and the culture as mirror them. In trying to escape the meaninglessness of daily American life, Chester Hunnicutt Pomeroy has become its personal embodiment. At one point after he has been interviewed by CBS News, Chester explains his schtick: "I explained that I considered that I represented not so much the middle of the republic that produced mass murderers but the part of the mass murderer who explained that he didn't mean anything, that he just wanted to get out of town. I pointed out that poison dripping from a fang reflected the world around it as well as a virgin's tear. . . . The commentator said he thought I was 'sick' and that my 'corruption' was surpassed only by the 'corruption' that had produced me" (75). The commentator's response explains exactly the bizarre predicament Chester finds himself in. It seems obvious to him that the society is corrupt; evidently normal people accept corruption as a fact and continue with their lives in a conventional manner, but Chester simply cannot: "Walking about as though nothing were wrong is just too studied for the alert" (86). Chester, then, has no respect for those who function in society without becoming discouraged. As he explains, "I stand for those who have made themselves up" (85). Thus, to combat the age, Chester begins to depict its atrocities in an effort to mirror reality for the unalert. Instead, the unalert love his act and make him a national hero. To compound the complexity of the situation, he loves being the center of attention and continues the act, believing his own game and personifying the culture he sought to expose.

If *Ninety-two in the Shade* echoes Hemingway, *Panama* evokes Fitzgerald. The most obvious comparison is that Chester imbues Catherine with the powers of salvation just as Gatsby empowers Daisy. But a more subtle comparison is apparent in that Gatsby and Chester play God when they reinvent themselves. Neither is the man he started out to be; both become the product of their own imaginations. Chester, since he is his own spokesperson, is more obvious. A heavy user of cocaine, he tells us early that those on coke think they are God (21), and that he sees himself as a sort of savior pouring blood from his head in an effort to reestablish the sense of human meaning and worth he feels society has lost (43).

It is Chester's concern with becoming a savior that explains his fascination with Jesse James, whose presence he continually invokes. On the one hand, James represents the same world as the mythic Pecos Bill (a McGuane symbol of transcendence in the earlier novels), a world of romance and adventure in which glorious heroes arrive on horseback wielding swords or Colt revolvers—the sort of world Chester's real or imagined grandfather represents when he appears on horseback, despairs of Chester's casual dress, and abandons all hope for future generations (121). No glory is possible in this Hotcakesland, where to savor a Big Mac is to live in the present (162), to embody the values of our time, as it were. On the other hand, Jesse James represents a hero as bogus as the sensationalized Chester (and by extension, as bogus as the culture that produced him). Jesse James was a guerrilla fighter, a robber and a killer, not the Robin Hood of the border country. And Chester is a performer of outlandish acts for money: he does not save the public from themselves but simply takes their money in exchange for providing them with vicarious fulfillment. Chester knows full well that real cowboys in our time are found in drugstores (145).

Unfortunately, Chester is for the most part a premature ejaculator (51) and endless masturbator (10, 55)—a basically ineffective and self-absorbed member of the age of narcissism—who falls victim to the age's relentless need for superficial titillation. When the public begins to tire of him, he becomes more and more outlandish, until he commits the almost-impossible act: in vomiting on the mayor of New York, he has achieved a plateau that even the age of tastelessness finds tasteless. Like Gatsby, the creature he has created goes out of control and destroys the possibility of achieving his original purpose.

When the public no longer craves him, Chester does not know what to do. He has, as it were, become what he pretended to be. Despite his professed need for a union with Catherine to achieve the salvation of normalcy, he cannot relinquish his penchant for outlandish acts. Even his efforts at winning Catherine seem dependent on his talent for going too far. In addition to nailing his hand to her door, he thinks about getting run over in front of her, and as a example of how he cannot escape the self he has become, he falls victim to a scheme involving the grave-robbed bones of a local hero. As Gatsby is required to be a criminal in order to become respectable, Chester is required to become base in order to be a savior—and in the end can save no one, not even himself. While Jesse James lives on in myth and mystery, Gatsby and Chester are confined to the residue of the ages that at once defined and destroyed them.

If *Panama* is not, as some reviewers claim, vintage McGuane, the explanation may lie in the minor characters. They are too much the embodiment of contemporary American culture to deserve compassion. To empathize with them, we would have to surrender to the same hopelessness and despair that swallow Chester. These characters are motivated by nothing but greed and pleasure. Even Susan Lardner's favorite, Marcelline, is essentially revolting. She is bisexual, having sex with Catherine, Chester, and numerous others. Sex for her is recreation, while she saves her "love" for a grave-robbing musician. Her inability to capture our concern may stem from her being too doped up most of the time to have much control over her actions. Like Chester, she simply is not confident of her own identity. As a consequence, all her actions appear selfish and without meaning.

Roxy, Chester's stepmother, who holds the deed to the family's waterfront property, will go to bed with anyone (13), even if it costs her the family money. The most compelling thing about Roxy is that she was once pronounced dead, a fact that greatly interests Chester. He would no doubt appreciate a firsthand report about death, because he has deduced that death is the only way he will ever escape the age that has already killed him without letting him actually die. Roxy does report to him, but Chester misses the point. If death has taught Roxy anything, it has taught her that there is more to life than Chester dreams of in his philosophy. At her finest moment, she tells him the truth about himself: "The world is full of things that are not awaiting your description" (164). That Chester need not combat or mirror the age all by himself is a truth Chester cannot accept.

Roxy's future husband, Curtis Peavy, will marry anyone who owns waterfront property. He is an attorney-businessman out for himself, a man who has sex with his secretary in a sleeping bag in Roxy's house and who is not above intimidating people who interfere with his goals. His strong-arm man, Nylon Pinder, has, as his name implies, a nylon backbone. The not-necessarily-macho Chester has no trouble physically dispatching him. As evidence of how nefarious Pinder is, he steals Chester's dog, a spotted beagle that has no name. The dog functions mostly as symbol: in this age, a man has no best friend he can call by name. When Chester does name the dog, he calls her Deirdre—after, we suspect, the princess in the Irish myth who kills herself following the murder of her husband. Like the denizens of Hotcakesland, the poor dog goes from nondescript to doomed. Although these characters may not be engaging, they are perfect representations of the age Pomeroy is raging against: predictable, selfish, mostly indistinguishable—not anybody we would want to know.

The characters who do, however, shed positive light on the situation and help make the novel as important as any in the McGuane canon are Chester's dead brother Jim, Catherine, a private eye named Don, and Chester's father. Brother Jim is a vague presence whose utterances were never clearly understood by Chester. We know that he maintained an innocence Chester had never developed (127), that he knew what ailed Chester but died without ever saying what that was (48), and that his sense of dying was that life continued without him (127). He was essentially a victim of the drug culture, one whose innocence left him unable to survive. The most quizzical of the passages regarding Jim occurs when Chester tells us his brother had "the sense of humor that is the mirror of pain, the perfect mirror, not the trick mirror of satirists" (45). The key here is the difference between satire and humor. Humor depicts what is funny in a situation for everyone to enjoy; satire mocks what is ridiculous at the expense of the mocked. Chester is a satirist: he does not desire that the public laugh at itself; he is attempting to engender self-revulsion, self-loathing. There is a considerable degree of empathy in humor; there is no empathy in Chester's public acts. He wants not to feel a part of the age, a part of the human race of his time. Jim knew people for who they are, could not take them seriously enough to mock them, and felt left out of the possibilities of life when he died. Chester, who has divorced himself from the race, would be glad of such a death. He has taken the age too seriously and allowed enmity to take control of him.

When we first see Catherine, Chester notes that her Rhonda Fleming eminence (6) is still intact. The reference to Fleming here is interesting. An actress from the fifties, a time when women's roles were conventional in the extreme, Fleming usually played women who either wound up with the hero or, more often, wished they did. A "girl" more for the fifties than the seventies, Catherine wants a traditional existence. When she leaves Chester, she tells him she is going to Panama because "in Panama I'm married. I have a man and he'll stand up for me through thick and thin" (174). Catherine thinks of herself not as a part of a whole couple but as an appendage to a man. Chester can hardly maintain himself, let alone stand up for "his woman" through good times and bad. In fact, because of Chester's raging philosophy, there have been none of the really prosperous times of the sort Catherine imagines. She will not respond to her frustration with the culture the same way Chester does. She knows contemporary life provides little hope for romance, but she continues to love Chester in the traditional way

(136). She evades the light (116), the plastic truth of the times. The best she can manage is to realize that she cannot face what's inside him (52) and therefore cannot help him (143). Just what it is about Catherine that Chester thinks is going to save him is not clear. He appears to be romanticizing the value she holds for his life in much the same way Gatsby idealizes Daisy. Romantic and idealized love, Chester's message seems to be, is enough to heal the wounds and change life. Even when his behavior strongly suggests that the ordinary is anathema to him, Chester claims to respect ordinary people (120) and to want a traditional family life with Catherine (145).

Don is a private detective Catherine employs to follow Chester and periodically remind him of his recent activities. Her hope is that the process will help restore Chester's ability to remember on his own. During one such briefing, Don also tells Chester the truth about himself: "Do you know how ugly it is not to give in to someone trying to save you" (151). Chester, however, does not want his memory restored. He feels his own energy dwelling with society's mindless mobs whose major dream is forgetfulness (166). Chester must flee Don because he knows the crowd has the right idea. To endure in our time is to live perpetually in the now. Americans cannot give credence to Chester's efforts, because showing people who they are in their worst moments does not accomplish their salvation. At one and the same time, Chester refuses his real-life savior, Don, and is himself the embodiment of a savior nobody desires.

This concern for saviors explains why Pomeroy prefers that Jesse James inhabit his father, "a happy man from Bunkersville, Ohio, who has made a fortune packaging snack foods" (142). Typical of McGuane protagonists in the early fiction, Chester is bothered by the security and ordinariness of his background; in this case, the security is even bunkered. He insists that his father is dead and refuses to let go of the notion that Jesse James lives. Instead of riches made from tasteless goodies shot full of preservatives, Chester sees his "family glories [as] the sound of horses in the underbrush, . . . gunpowder in percussion Colts, tired men in their hangouts, haunted Missouri barns" (152). But Chester's father surmounts this mythology and forces a reconciliation. Chester knows that all his father desires is for Chester to say hello, to acknowledge him as his father; after that they can go their own ways, knowing there will be more time later to say what needs to be said. But Chester ends the novel wishing "there was not so much time" (175). Admitting that his father lives will require acknowledging that the savior figure Jesse James embodies for him is nonexistent. Chester will have to accept himself for who he is: the son of an unillustrious packager of

snack foods, an appropriate symbol of life in unromanticized and unideal-
ized Hotcakesland.

   This failure of romanticism explains the frustration Chester feels with his
times. As a child he had imagined going to sea—a McGuane symbol of
transcendent reality—because of a movie he saw (67). At another point the
sea and hoofbeats (Jesse James and, in the earlier novels, Pecos Bill) merge
in his mind (146–47). The adulthood he has achieved is not the idealized
adulthood he imagined as a boy. Instead of accepting life on its own terms
he combats life through romanticism, idealizing himself this time as Jesse
James: "I know that Jesse robbed and killed and that he was lonely" (157).
On this level Chester is the lone rider righting the wrongs of society. But the
problem is that he is ineffectual. He desires to carry a gun at a time when
snack food is the best weapon for keeping the wolf from the door.

   Chester is a man whose imagined code of conduct no longer holds sway, a
point we understand when he explains that downtown Key West is always
changing: "Today an old family jewelry store had become a moped rental
shop; a small bookstore where Hart Crane and Stephen Crane had momentarily coexisted on a mildewed shelf was now an electric griddle warming a
stack of pre-fab tortillas" (165). He may persist in thinking that there was a
time when the glories of Jesse James triumphed, but now reality is simply a
series of shifting foundations. In fact, reality may have always been shifty.
Chester reports that coke spoons have been found on a sunken Spanish gal-
leon and wonders what that says about the golden age of Spain (92). What
it says is that life probably never has been romantic and ideal, so cope with
it. Survival, if it is to come, will come in conventional ways. When his father
offers conventional familial love, Chester seems resigned but not eager to accept this love. Chester expects God will save him in the end (86), but precisely who is Chester's God is unclear; language, however, will help ease the
burden—the age will never totally obliterate anyone who can say, "I want to
garner kudos by manufacturing an artificial paradise of household materials" (72). Without realizing it, Chester has pointed up the key to his own
well-being. What he seems to need to learn and live with is that it is the
common, not the romanticized, materials of life from which human beings
derive ultimate meaning. As the novel ends he is beginning to realize the
unillustrious course of true life, but he is not eager to accept such a reality.

   And indeed, perhaps he never will. A McGuane protagonist to the core,
Chester Hunnicutt Pomeroy may well die trying (174) to achieve his imagined place in his imagined world. At one point, he suggests decoding the
sky (66), the home of Pecos Bill. If Chester continues to think he can discover answers in the stars, he will never be ready to live conventional life on

earth. At another point, Chester ponders the conclusion of the Classic Comic edition of James Fenimore Cooper's *The Prairie*. In Cooper's story, the law of the frontier is cruel yet just, and the possibilities of the prairie are endless and open (79). In Hotcakesland America, there is no law of the frontier. Because Chester's age has too many choices, too much ambiguity, and too much potential for the insane and bizarre, he prefers the comic-book version. He sees hope in cutting his losses and starting over (59). Unwilling to acknowledge that life is determined by forces out of his control, he maintains a habit of abandoning people who do not suit him (73).

That Chester simply cannot exhibit grace under pressure is underscored when he overhears two retired New Yorkers exchange lines from Hemingway's *The Sun Also Rises,* the ones about how pretty it is to think that Jake and Brett could have had "such a damned good time together" (136). Chester cannot content himself with imagining this good time but must make the effort to achieve it. Even though he appears to have acknowledged his rightful father as the novel ends, he gives no indication that he can gracefully cope with the limitations of reality (175).[8] He may not have the resolve to declare himself "at large" like Nicholas Payne, but he has not admitted defeat. Like McGuane's later novels *Something to Be Desired* and *Keep the Change, Panama* ends at a lull in the protagonist's activities, rather than on a resolution of the concerns created from his romanticized ideals for himself.

Chapter Seven

Nobody's Angel: High Plains Drifter

Overview

Nobody's Angel left no doubt that Thomas McGuane's career as a strictly comic novelist had come to an end. Even he does not see the thrust of the novel to be essentially comic. He wrote out of the ache created when his father, mother, and sister died: "I was in a really gloomy period and was interested in the more fatalistic elements of life." McGuane found himself controlled by the book. He could not tear himself away from the writing, even though it fueled his depression. The writing was "hard bitten"—the going difficult, the revising hard. Even though a substantial number of readers continue to claim *Nobody's Angel* is McGuane's best book, he has not looked at the novel in years: "There's this depressing fatalism about it which very much belongs to that time in my life. I don't repudiate that at all. It's just that the possibilities of life seem so much brighter to me now."

Nobody's Angel is McGuane's first book set entirely in the contemporary West and the first to fictionalize Livingston into Deadrock. The protagonist, Patrick Fitzpatrick, resigns his commission as an army tank commander in Europe to return to the family ranch in Montana. While in Europe he idealizes ranch life, but once he has actually returned, he is at a loss as to what to do with himself. His father is dead, his mother departed. His grandfather mopes around, lost in reveries of the past. His sister, depressed and mentally ill, leaves her Indian lover, David Catches, and returns to the ranch to commit suicide. The most meaningful relationship Patrick has is with his mare Leafy.

Because of his skill at horse training, Patrick is engaged by Tio and Claire Burnett to train a stallion. Tio and Claire are Oklahomans summering in Montana. Tio is an ersatz good old boy whose high-finance fast-talking first confuses and then bores Patrick; Claire is a Fitzgeraldian creature who totally captures Patrick's imagination. Patrick and Claire charge toward an inevitable affair that gives Patrick thoughts of true love and a new life. By the novel's end, Patrick's world has become totally engulfed in confusion. Tio dies, Claire terminates their affair without affection, and Patrick abandons the ranch, moves to Spain, and undertakes an alcohol-engulfed fantasy existence.

Critical Reception

Nobody's Angel met with mixed reviews. Generally, reviewers chose one of two responses: (a) they awarded McGuane varied marks for reaching into new territory, or (b) they admitted they were simply tired of him and his protagonist. Many noticed that the McGuane hero really does not change; he is usually the erratic son of wealthy parents who has no interest in conventional life. Rightly or wrongly, most reviewers assumed that this character reflects McGuane himself. Several noticed that McGuane's prose best distinguishes itself when he writes about horses.

In the *National Review,* Jeffrey Brodrick reviews McGuane's record as a master of preposterous contrivance and clever utterance who creates life-size puppets who do little more than the author's bidding. Brodrick then points out that McGuane has now created three characters who have slipped away to achieve a life of their own: David Catches, Tio, and Patrick's grandfather. Brodrick sees McGuane becoming more tender and vulnerable and excuses the novel's misses as the awkwardness of a first attempt to write serious fiction that is not dwarfed by its own dependence on comic violence and clever language. The review ends positively, pointing out that McGuane is a "monstrous talent [who is] starting to get real."[1]

The *New Yorker,* however, sees nothing remarkable in the novel. A lone and unsigned paragraph in "Books Briefly Noted" finds the work nothing more than a film script and the story tired nihilism.[2] Ken Tucker's review in the *Village Voice* is practically abusive. McGuane is immersing his readers in "some pretty highbrow horse shit."[3] The book is not too deficient, as Thomas McGuane novels go, until the author overreaches for a lyrical climax—certainly not as unsatisfactory as *Panama* or *Ninety-two in the Shade,* which Tucker sees as solipsistic and mannered. Tio is an interesting character who, Tucker thinks, allows McGuane to satirize his own protagonist, but Tucker is not sure that McGuane really knows what his own character is doing.

Notices in *Time* and *Newsweek* are ambivalent. *Time's* Richard Stengel credits McGuane with burying the West's romantic myths but concludes that novels demonstrating more affection for horses than people tend to "pull up lame."[4] Ray Sawhill, in the other weekly, sees McGuane attempting for the first time to bring direct emotion into his work. McGuane, however, does not go far enough, because he is essentially an ironist and his efforts at sincerity embarrass his readers.[5]

In a longer notice in the *Nation,* Geoffrey Stokes points out that for the first time since *The Sporting Club,* the McGuane protagonist has returned to whiskey addiction. Thus, *Nobody's Angel* is about hangovers—crippling hangovers demonstrating that "short-term pleasures guarantee long-term pain."[6] This insight is important because Stokes asserts that Patrick Fitzpatrick is not the usual outlandish McGuane protagonist; he is crazy in normal ways, ways that remind us of ourselves. Stokes sees the Patrick-Claire affair as an authentic love story, one that actual adults might experience. They cannot, of course, come to a happily-ever-after conclusion, because this is serious fiction and McGuane is a serious writer. Patrick and Claire must answer for the consequences of their actions. Essentially, Stokes credits McGuane with beginning to fulfill his earlier promise of becoming a significant American writer.

Stokes's most useful insight lies in his praise of McGuane for transcending black humor: "His characters make their jokes not because the world is about to come to a messy end all over them but because it just may not and one might as well have as good a time as possible" (342). Stokes indicates here a new phase in McGuane's writing: McGuane is indeed beginning to become "real." As Gary Fisketjon so aptly points out in his review of *Panama,* McGuane is beginning to abandon the easy cleverness of a "smart-ass" who really does not care if the world destroys itself; he is beginning to demonstrate the wisdom necessary to continue living in a world that is just as absurd as it has always been but that shows no signs of blowing itself up and leaving protagonists to eternal peace.

Vance Bourjaily, in the *New York Times Book Review,* analyzes Fitzpatrick within the European tradition of the superfluous man. Bourjaily's conclusion is that the Europeans were "far more cynical, elegant and aloof," while Patrick is more vulnerable and less foolish, thus showing McGuane to be "a thoroughly American writer of his time."[7] He also sees McGuane maturing. Although the old bizarre episodes remain important to the script, Bourjaily senses a new depth of feeling: McGuane gives the reader doses of rage and pathos at a depth he has not heretofore reached. Bourjaily concludes by asserting that the novel's sometimes oblique and elliptical stretches are worth the effort to understand them because *Nobody's Angel* is McGuane's "best book so far, and he is a very good writer indeed" (9).

A Reading

Nobody's Angel depicts the failure of romanticism as a way of life. In addition to demonstrating that the West of our imaginations—and whatever romantic and glorious exploits it may inspire—has come to an end, the novel demonstrates the inability of individuals to discover purpose, achieve fulfillment, and register an impact on the flow of human events. Above all, the book articulates the impossibility of happy endings. McGuane lets us know early that the contemporary West is wrecked. The farmer-operators pack "the protein off the land," and the cowboys are "often very lazy white men" (3). The state motto, ORO Y PLATE, "shows a real go-getter attitude" (49). The people in control are those who have come only to harvest gold and silver, not to partake of the West's "dopey complacency" and achieve selfhood under the big sky.

Patrick Fitzpatrick is dislocated. He has been a tank captain in the army for his entire adult life, and the only place he feels secure is inside his womb-like tank. He suffers from "sadness-for-no-reason" (61). He has returned to the family ranch, where his sister and grandfather still live, and found "it was edges and no middle" (61). He feels "stranded on the beautiful ranch he [will] someday own, land, homestead, water rights, cattle and burden" (65). The word *burden* here places Fitzpatrick in the company of the earlier McGuane protagonists. He is destined for respectability, but becoming a property owner is not a meaningful achievement for him. Fitzpatrick sees the ranch as a burden because he has "no idea what he [will] do with it" (65). Simply beginning a conventional existence and routinely working the ranch seem out of the question.

The ranch has no middle, because Fitzpatrick's family is in a shambles. His pilot father is dead. His mother has another son in California, where she now lives, married to an unremarkable man. His sister Mary, for whom he cares deeply, is insane. And his grandfather has grown old and useless, dreaming of the West of his youth while approaching death in a modern West he cannot respect. We begin to understand when Fitzpatrick wonders whether his own suffering is not from "the jaggedness-of-the-everyday" (60). His life has no meaning; the events of his life add up to nothing.

One of the major holes in Patrick's life seems to have been created by his parents' failure to be parents. His mother and father were violent adversaries in a household where strife was natural and normal. At one point during an argument, Patrick's father angrily destroyed plumbing with a duck gun (132). While they were growing up, Patrick and Mary were always apprehensively waiting for the next explosion. After his mother remarries and moves away, she is little more than extraneous noise in Patrick's existence. Rather than demonstrating love and support, she is unsympathetic toward Mary and appears mostly annoyed with her first husband's family. Patrick sees his father's death as abandonment. He wonders how he can be alive if his father is dead (21); he charges that his father "left him as crow bait" (86). Patrick is guilty here of placing too much pressure on his need for his father. It is almost as if he were making his father's death an excuse for not attempting to generate meaning in his own life. Ultimately, he admits his father was not "so terrific" but achieved importance only by dying (133). Patrick has attached his need for a reason to live to his father. The truth is that there was little serious understanding between father and son. Were the man still alive, he could not end Patrick's sadness-for-no-reason. Patrick continues to search for a foundation that has real meaning, a foundation he cannot identify.

Mary, too, falls victim to the concept of jaggedness-of-the-everyday because she has "an insufficient resistance to pain of every kind" (109). She is a recipient of the family's "recurring mental illness" (104). She has sought meaning in life without knowing what she was seeking (25). Drugs continue to control her; she has tried prostitution. For a time she lives a stable existence with David Catches: "We had a trailer house down in the trees. We had a good dog and four saddle horses. We were happy" (117). But the relationship doesn't save her from emptiness. She is too self-absorbed and defeated, too passive to fulfill a partner's role in the relationship. Mary is pregnant with David's baby and commits suicide as if bringing new life into the world is an act of affirmation she cannot make. In an emotional outburst after her funeral service, Patrick passes judgment on her life and death: "[She] was an unhappy girl and she isn't going anywhere" (115). This modern West holds promise for neither the young nor the dead.

Mary is as enigmatic as Patrick. Her sadness-for-no-reason is explained as inherited insanity, but her behavior appears to be the result of drug burnout. In either case, her motivations are beyond the power of reason. She is, in the most romantic sense, hopelessly doomed. If her life is unlivable, Mary's only recourse—at least in a romantic landscape—is suicide. Suicide, of course, is the last great romantic act, the individual's ultimate assertion of self-reliance, her effort to triumph over life, to end the pain. That she is a former prostitute named for the Virgin Mother contributes the final twist of hopeless irony to her failure to find meaning in life. Both Madonna and Magdalen, but in the final analysis concretely neither, she cannot find peace.

What Patrick and David Catches finally realize is that regardless of romantic myths about the powers of macho men in the West, they themselves simply do not have the power to save her. Catches invests great faith in the saving powers of love and takes umbrage when Patrick asserts that Indians are supposed to know that life has no meaning (135). The fact is that Catches thought love could save Mary. He had done everything right. They did not have much money, but they set up housekeeping and undertook the simple pleasures of companionship, reading, cooking, raising a few animals. Catches was happy, but ultimately Mary left him—the last time for good. Mary did not fulfill the demands of his simple romanticism. The one shred of evidence that allows Catches to rise above utter despair is that he knows Mary meant more to him than she did to Patrick (136). Catches has maintained the ideal, kept to the rigors of his own idealized code. But his code has achieved no impact on contemporary reality.[8]

The old, as well, secure no place in McGuane's wrecked West. Patrick's grandfather has "nighthawked on the biggest of the northern ranches, [has] seen gunfighters in their dotage, [has] run this ranch like an old time cowman's outfit" (61), but "[t]here's nothing to do anymore" (124). The West has changed, and everything from sonic booms to valleys cluttered with yard lights has depressed the old man. The only things he feels positive about are Australia, which he has heard is open country like Montana once was, and western movies. A not-entirely-defeated version of Pecos Bill, the old man still has "small wings on his shoes" (16), but he has gone from real ranching to full-time ranging in the romantic West of his mind.

His most hopeful fit of excitement comes when he auditions to be an extra in a western about to be filmed locally. Yet even that brings overtones of sadness and ends in disappointment. The film is *Hondo's Last Move,* evocative of a never-never-land West popularized by John Wayne and Louis L'Amour. Even then, the "last move" of the title hints at the dying of the West and maybe even Hondo himself. We will never know, because the project does not materialize. The distributor forsakes westerns for science fiction. Even on the movie screen, Grandfather's West has vanished. In the end, the old man moves into town and takes an apartment from which he can see "the Emperial Theater and the Hawk, a little bar that sold cheese and cigars" (174). To solidify the image of Grandfather alone with his memories, McGuane tells us that on his last hunt the old man "shot the best elk of his life, [which Patrick arranges to have] mounted and hung in the Hawk" (226). The open West has been reduced to one-bedroom apartments, yesterday's movies, and mounted animals. The movies and the animals serve only as reminders of a glorious West of the popular imagination. The West McGuane evokes here is weakened by a romanticism that idealizes both the past and the present. Grandfather Fitzpatrick may represent a finer, truer time, but in reality he simply represents a different time. He copes with a present in which he feels foreign by idealizing the past, a past that ultimately never was.

Tio, on the other hand, idealizes the present, a West of jet-setters whose newfound wealth confounds their own sense of the real. Not a genuine stockman like Patrick's grandfather, Tio is mainly interested in oil, cattle futures, row crops, and running horses. Since Tio's main hobby is pretending to be a good old boy, Fitzpatrick sees him as a personification of the wrecked West, a West with "gangrene" (38). The West is the new Garden of Eden where the apples are golden and plentiful, not because it allows people to flourish in natural harmony with the processes of ranch and family life but because it makes them richer than their wildest expectations. The contemporary West of McGuane's vision is not the wild and woolly, "raggedy-assed West" in need of taming; it is a West that destroys people—as it does Tio—from the inside out because the human mechanism loses the sense of its own humanness.

There is, then, not much in McGuane's Montana to help Patrick Fitzpatrick overcome his sadness-for-no-reason. His major hope lies in his love affair with Claire Burnett. Tio, eager to gallivant around the country looking after his properties, enlists Patrick to stay close to the ranch and serve as protector for Claire (58). When Patrick and Claire begin an unstoppable love affair, Patrick takes stock of his life and invests their affair with great meaning: "Claire could change it all" (137). He is touched by David Catches's love for Mary and seeks the same intensity with Claire. He sees himself "a sap of the heart" (147) and wishes theirs "could be a big simp love story" (147), the kind found in romantic books. Patrick thinks of their affair in the same way that his grandfather remembers the old West: a place where survival and fulfillment are possible. Patrick desires to find in Claire "a sense of purpose" (150). He attempts to enlist her help in becoming the creator of his own escape from sadness-for-no-reason.

But Claire will not become a part of Patrick's romanticized scenario. Her commitment to Tio transcends Patrick's ability to understand. Her family provided the money for her and Tio's life-style; Tio's people are actually poor Okies (192). This discrepancy in their backgrounds has driven Tio insane, and Claire blames herself (191). Tio now suffers from incurable delusions of grandeur, and Claire has promised she will not abandon him (202). Even though she appears honestly in love with Patrick, she never stops loving Tio, and Patrick's imagined new life is simply that: imagined. Even when Tio dies, Claire will not marry Patrick. She makes love to him one last time, accentuating that it is the final time. She becomes hard and tells

Patrick that love is "nothing you can do anything with" (225) and that it
never can be all that matters to her, because she "set out to have been
around" (225). Claire must be strident to make her point, because when it
comes to his dream of living happily ever after with her, Patrick will not take
no for an answer. But Claire does not share Patrick's romantic view of their
affair.

The conflict can be seen in this exchange between Patrick and Claire:

"Does one ever just say the hell with it?"
"The hell with what?" she asked.
"The consequences."
"Some people do," she said, without much warmth for those people. (205).

Consequences have no credibility in Patrick's idealized notion of the life he
seeks. He has lived without regard to consequences. He resigned from the
army without thinking of his career or his pension. Just as he is unequipped
to understand his dead sister or the demise of his grandfather's West, so is
he unable to comprehend Claire's attitudes about love and their relationship. He has also abandoned without a real backward glance whatever life
he was actually living in Europe. His relationships were ultimately shallow;
he thinks of his lovers there as 20 vulvae (134). He returned to Montana to
rescue the dying ranch but in truth hoped the ranch would rescue him. He
quests to save his sister but really does not know her well enough to understand where to begin. The only thing he really manages to do is help his
grandfather find an apartment; he is more successful with the ending of the
old than with the beginning of the new.

The difficulty with Patrick's quest is that idealized adventures require the
cooperation of other players if they are to succeed. He would like to begin
life again with Claire, to fully achieve the meaning he idealistically believes
is possible when one is truly in love. Claire, however, will not act according
to his rules: the consequences are too dire. Although she gives him a picture
of herself, he does not keep it, for it reminds him of the impossibility of his
romantic dream. His attraction to the ache of jazz bebop drives him more
deeply into himself, making him feel "like the Ancient Mariner at an abandoned bus stop" (217).

Claire, on the other hand, is a victim of her own version of romanticism.
Even though the excuse for her affair with Patrick is that she was simply
seeking experience, we can imagine that she may well love Patrick but not in
a way that commits her to him so that he can live happily ever after. In fact,
Tio claims her idealism. She feels responsible for turning Tio into the ersatz

high roller he is. By extension, she feels responsible for his disintegration. Tio, because of his own notion of who he needs to be to please her and her family, has tried to turn himself into something he is not, and the effort has produced epilepsy and suicide. While she can be practical with Patrick, Claire succumbs to the romanticist's guilt where her husband is concerned. (At one point she claims her affair with Patrick killed Tio [224].) Once she capitulates to guilt, she eliminates any possibility for future happiness from their affair. Indeed, all her future love affairs run the risk of being rendered ineffectual by her guilt over Tio.[9]

In the end, Patrick survives but not in the West. When he was a teenager, Patrick invented an imaginary girlfriend named Marion Easterly to camouflage nights of hell-raising. Even though he was eventually found out, the fantasy remains a part of his consciousness. His sister claims "that Marion had been his greatest love, that no one would ever equal her in Patrick's eyes" (183). Though he had hoped Claire would replace Marion, a living woman will never become the woman of a man's imagination, and when Claire dismisses him, Patrick rejoins the army and achieves fulfillment within his fantasy: the word "from someone who knew someone who knew someone [is] that he [has] a woman in Madrid, an American named Marion Easterly" (227). The word also is that when they are together, Patrick is "a bit of a blackout drinker" (227).

An irony exists in the name Marion Easterly. Marion is the adjectival form of Mary, which could either indicate Patrick's affection for his sister or represent the purity of his fantasy. Patrick was an adolescent when he created Marion, and his belief that he could live happily ever after with Claire, regardless of the realities of her situation, is a purely adolescent notion. His imagined Marion provides the blind love Patrick could never receive from Claire. Then too, the -ion spelling is generally used to indicate males and supports the idea that Marion is a male fantasy. The name Easterly indicates the direction of Patrick's ultimate fantasy—the walk-up in Castille. Here, of course, McGuane is casting his protagonist against type. Fulfillment in the West does not come from yearning to go East. If the old axiom "west to the future, east toward culture" can be believed, we can assume that as long as Patrick remains locked in his fantasylike, idealized view of the world, he has no real future. And, the novel seems to say, having no future is acceptable to Patrick because personal fulfillment is not possible in the contemporary West of Thomas McGuane. Patrick has returned to what is left of the frontier and failed to generate a new beginning because he has understood all along that the sort of book romance he seeks is not possible (147).

The secret to understanding Patrick is in realizing that he is a whiskey addict. What we see in the novel is the unfocused, energyless world of the alcoholic. Patrick is depressed, supposedly for no reason—that is, no reason he can think of—because he is not free of the effects of the alcohol in his blood. Whiskey is always between Patrick and real life. He can move by fits and starts, but he cannot liberate himself to live any more successfully than his sister could escape her addiction. He has lost his will to battle for survival; that is one reason consequences mean nothing to him. He will dream of a life with Claire, but he will not fight for it. They correspond for a time, but he stops responding (227). He gives her Leafy, ultimately not so much as a gift as to rid his life of the one relationship that seems to have concrete meaning. The horse, a living and breathing being, is Patrick's one link to reality. At the same time, and ironically, horses, seen at one point with stars on their backs and with no legs on the ground (130), appear to be the only celestial (read transcendent) beings in the novel. In giving away Leafy Patrick says good-bye to the West. With Claire and Leafy behind him, he can sink completely into his fantasy world, where consequences are of no concern.

Indeed, the only time Patrick Fitzpatrick resembles a real Western hero—one in the mold of the transcendent Pecos Bill or the fictional Jesse James—is when he is breaking Leafy. He is firm but gentle, knowing, and thorough. Once the task is accomplished, he says, "I love this scene. It has no booze or women in it" (20). Real life, however, because it is full of booze and women, is much more complex—to the point of meaninglessness. Patrick's goals are muddy, his vision impaired.

His two boldest actions demonstrate how little in control of himself Patrick is. In a supermarket parking lot he declares war on the yuppies who are changing the West. He crawls atop an all-terrain vehicle and barks at a malamute-German shepherd named Dirk until the dog tears up the vehicle's interior in a frenzy. After the "extraordinarily well groomed" (76) owners return, Dirk and Patrick stare each other to a standstill, a shoot-out avoided only when the owner gains control of the dog. It is, in Patrick's mind, "perhaps the number-one Man-Versus-Animal deal for many years here in the Rockies" (78). In reality, of course, the whole incident is silly. The yuppie couple have not been harming anyone—except that their presence signals the end of the working-cowboy West Patrick's grandfather longs for—and Patrick has been simply obnoxious.

Patrick's greatest venture into heroism concerns Deke Patwell, the local newspaper editor, who has been sensationalizing the lives of Patrick's family. Patrick has been pictured drunk on page 1 and—the last straw—Patrick's outburst at Mary's funeral has been satirized in print. McGuane may be indulging himself a bit here, since Patwell's newspaper appears to be more of a scandal sheet of the sort that dogged McGuane through his highly public film years, rather than the usual slow-moving and benevolent small-town newspaper, but whether the author is indulging himself in a private revenge has little impact on the narrative. Patwell is clearly a villain who deserves the caning Patrick gives him. The incident has classic heroic overtones in that Patrick must venture into Patwell's home country—the newspaper office—and carry out his mission in front of Patwell's own forces—in this case, frightened reporters and secretaries. McGuane is conscious that such behavior may be the only act of heroism possible in the contemporary West. When the police arrive, not to rescue the hero but to save the villain, the text explains, "It was turning into a western" (140).

Sadly, horses and not men are the only elements that seem to make the West western in the heroic sense. The most damning evidence is the appearance of two West Coast hunters who arrive on the scene to set a new record in the murdering of coyotes. Wired on amphetamines, they lure coyotes with recorded rabbit sounds and then terrorize the animals in their landscape-ravaging Land Cruiser. In real life these men are a sheetrocker and a perfataper (184)—uninspiring occupations at best. Like Patrick Fitzpatrick, who is not important enough for anything to happen to (197), they are heroes in a West with no place for heroics: "The West's last stands were less and less appropriate to epic poetry and murals" (223).

Nobody's Angel announces the arrival of Thomas McGuane's fictional sensibility in the contemporary West some 15 years after he actually began living there. His western film scripts seem to be light rehearsals. In *Nobody's Angel* he rids the landscape of romanticism, both ancient and modern. Those tied to any sort of romantic ideal cannot survive in the contemporary West. When Patrick and Catches are discussing the deceased Mary, McGuane says, "[T]he stars crowded down upon them" (129). Indeed, in McGuane's West the big sky is little (78) and inhuman (30). The heavens are too close for comfort; no transcendent presence is available to rescue these characters. The West of infinite possibility is no more available to the grandfathers who long for a more imaginary time than it is for the Tios who see the wide-open spaces as an unlimited Monopoly board. The addicts Patrick and Mary miss the possibilities of the big-sky country, as do those like Claire, who seek experience at other people's expense. Even people like David Catches, who seek fulfillment in simple pleasures, appear to be doomed. It is essentially a West where renewing rituals never occur (134), where everybody is nobody's angel and the jaggedness-of-the-everyday prevails.

Chapter Eight
Something to Be Desired:
From Son to Father

Overview

Strangely enough, *Something to Be Desired* remains a book about which Thomas McGuane is uncertain: "My most serious readers claim it as their favorite book. I don't see why. I guess it is a book that was written from such a deep place I don't really know what its objective features are." What is attractive is that in *Something to Be Desired,* the McGuane protagonist combines both conventional and unconventional goals. Lucien Taylor, a foreign service official in Central America, grows tired of normalcy and walks out on his wife, Suzanne, and son, James, to return to Montana and Emily, the lust object of his college years. But Emily has to flee because she has just murdered her surgeon husband. When she leaves her ranch in Lucien's care, he develops its sulfur spring into a thriving health spa. In no time, he becomes rich. Even though McGuane continues to maneuver his protagonist through some outlandish adventures because of an unbridled sexual appetite, he imbues Lucien with a sense of purpose higher than sport or making the world tense. Once his new wealth requires the reestablishment of order into his life, Lucien begins to want this family back.

Critical Response

On publication, *Something to Be Desired* did not receive the same notice as the earlier McGuane novels. The *New Yorker* and *Time* did not review it, and *Newsweek* gave it a scant 100 words under the heading "Footnotes." The *Newsweek* reviewer does, however, make two important points, saying that (a) McGuane is now writing with a tone of "chastened machismo" and (b) "those who praised McGuane's first books and then wrote him off should look again. He's still a contender."[1] In the *New York Times Book Review,* Robert Roper begins by proclaiming the novel McGuane's best, "a re-

markable work of honest colors and fresh phrasings that deliver strong,
earned emotional effects."[2] Roper's most insightful comment is this:

What we have in Thomas McGuane is a writer whose comic gifts . . . cause him to
write a prose too inherently lively, too highly colored for the tragic effects that
he—as a literary son of Hemingway—feels belong in serious books. As a result,
some of his earlier novels, such as *Ninety-two in the Shade,* are marred by a grafting
on of violent, *mano a mano* incidents, as if Mr. McGuane had lost faith in his own
technique—his dead on, wonderfully comic writing—to carry a weight of darker
meanings. But in *Something to Be Desired,* he overcomes this tendency. (11)

Roper seems to be saying that McGuane has become a kind of literary
adult, in that Lucien Taylor's struggle is not with other men but with himself. His goal is not any sort of victory over somebody or something; rather,
it is the achievement, through sometimes very conventional sources, of personal meaning. And Roper is right about the joy of McGuane's comedy—a
sense of fun missing from both *Panama* and *Nobody's Angel.* In this later
work McGuane peppers his narrative with comic relief. At one point, for instance, an errant tampon comes to rest on an unsuspecting windshield and
doggedly defies all the efforts of windshield wipers to dispatch it.[3] And
pointed juxtaposition appears throughout; for example, when one character
notes that death "is a long tunnel aimed at cheerful light" (115), Lucien
wonders if he has missed a television special on death—an unlikely source
of serious inquiry. We need not, then, find Lucien's quest for life's meaning
as oppressive and hopeless as it is for Chester Pomeroy or Patrick
Fitzpatrick.

A Reading

In *Something to Be Desired* McGuane departs from the claustrophobic
world of *Nobody's Angel* and champions a course for infinite possibility in
the twentieth-century American West. He also places this narrative in
Deadrock, thereby staking his claim to his own postage stamp of ground
and proclaiming himself a self-conscious son of Faulkner. Ironically, Deadrock here connotes none of the depression of *Nobody's Angel* and is actually
more of a Livingston[e]. Only at first glance does the novel appear to be the
usual blend of McGuane concerns. Lucien is another protagonist who grows
tired of normalcy and destroys his perfectly fine life with self-absorbed, erratic behavior. He is, as his name suggests, a regular devil. And once his new
life becomes empty, he, like Chester Pomeroy, tries to reform by reuniting

with his abandoned wife, Suzanne. But new and important elements contribute to the hope present in this story. McGuane provides Lucien with a son, James, and we see clearly that the fulfilling existence Lucien seeks—a stable family life—is a real possibility within the novel, not just a goal imagined by a hopelessly lost protagonist.

Important too is that Lucien's plight is not the result of his confronting pointless conformity; he is victimized by his penis, which drags him places he would never go alone and causes him shame (145). That McGuane allows his protagonist to be shamed by his own irresponsible behavior is hope in itself. The McGuane protagonist appears to have determined what sort of adult he intends to be. Unlike Vernor Stanton and Nicholas Payne, he is now after something other than manic adventuring. In fact, he is actually questing after middle-class stability. The "something" to be desired in the title sets up a trail of multiple meanings. It indicates the lack in Lucien's character: as a person, he "leaves something to be desired." When he abandons his marriage, he leaves something that he will come to desire. The woman he leaves his family for, of course, is something he desires at the time, and ultimately, the something to be desired comes to mean the fulfilling family life Lucien hopes to re-create.

Unlike most of McGuane's other protagonists—the notable exception is Tom Skelton in *Ninety-two in the Shade*—Lucien is not rebelling against stable parents. His own parents are anything but stable; indeed, in this novel the protagonist's isolation and bewilderment begin in the home. *Something to Be Desired* opens with a young Lucien and his father embarked on a camping trip in—fittingly—the Crazy Mountains. We sense immediately that the boy's parents are separated and that Lucien's father may even have possession of the boy illegally (3). A single sentence explains the father's irresponsible behavior: "His father had returned after hiding from his mother, hiding in, of all places, Arequipa, Peru, where he had cooked on sheep dung and drunk too much and mailed deranged letters to his son until his son flunked his courses and got kicked off the baseball team" (3). Not only has the father gone to exotic lengths to be away from his family, but he has also selfishly tried to maintain control over his son in a manner that has made normal life impossible for Lucien. In this scene Lucien's father is lost, and only by accident do they find their way back to camp. In a symbolic sense, the man, because he is lost in life, can provide no useful guidance to his son.

The father has also contributed to Lucien's notion of his penis as a separate being that cannot be controlled. They return from the camping trip and spend the night in a motel in Deadrock before presenting themselves to

Lucien's mother. Lucien wakes in the night to the scene of his father order-
ing from the room a strange woman who is hastily attempting to get back
into her clothes. The father explains and excuses his behavior in terms of the
boy's childhood pets: "we are all animals" (15). Once they are again in the
family home, Lucien learns that the initial separation was the result of his
mother's love affair with a good friend of his father's. Sexual fidelity, which
would require discipline, is never modeled for the child by either parent.

Lucien's inability to cope with marriage and responsibility can be attributed to the picture of life he receives from his parents. Affection seems not
to be part of Taylor life. His father rarely spends time with Lucien, and
when he does he clearly feels guilty about it (10). Lucien receives no support
for his values; for example, although he loves the Crazy Mountains, his father thinks they are useless—and by association, worthless (9). His mother
drinks all day and by evening finds her son a "prize boob" (21). The most
serious negative impact on Lucien is the adversarial relationship between his
father and mother. His father is a self-forgiver who thinks the world is
against him, a bit of self-aggrandizement his mother sees as simple coward-
ice in the face of life (6). Family "disputes" end with his father striking his
mother (17). This tendency toward violence and his inclination to call his
wife Momma indicate that Lucien's father is a perpetual adolescent, seemingly uncomfortable with the responsibilities of being a husband and a father. Lucien seems to have behaved in a similar fashion during his marriage.
He admits he did not really love Suzanne until their union was dissolved,
and he does not really want James until he no longer has him. Lucien simply
was not raised to appreciate life with a wife and a son.

Any sense of sexual discipline Lucien might have developed despite his
parents would have been impossible to maintain in college once he met
Emily, a young woman from his hometown: "Emily had no idea who Lucien
was. By way of compensation, she slept with him on their first meeting"
(23). Emily is engaged to a medical student and continues sexual relationships with both young men at the same time. From the beginning, Emily
will accept life only on her own terms. Eventually, she is abused by her surgeon husband and develops a hard resolve to survive. As an adult, she is totally self-absorbed and manipulating. Emily is a woman as selfish as Claire
appears in the conclusion to *Nobody's Angel,* and she continues her self-
absorbed actions throughout the novel, manipulating everyone, including
Lucien. At the same time he was involved with Emily, Lucien was dating
Suzanne. If Emily is darkness, Suzanne is light: "She took the position that
this was a decent world for an honest player" (25). This basic decency of
being is what Lucien eventually comes to value, and he marries Suzanne;

however, decency is not enough. Lucien is troubled by the "lack of high romance in his life" (26). He seems to be missing an element of fulfillment
that Suzanne and their young son, James, cannot provide. He has already
fallen victim to his penis and has been sexually active with co-workers and
whores. Suzanne sums up his attraction to Emily by calling her the queen of
whores (27), an assertion borne out when, on her penultimate appearance
in the novel, Emily sleeps naked next to her purse (171).

That Emily is a self-absorbed whore indicates McGuane's contention
that some girls-of-your-dreams are not worth dreaming about. Ann (*Bushwhacked Piano*) and Claire (*Nobody's Angel*) certainly are not. Lucien has
dreamed of Emily since their first encounter. Even though he races to Montana to rescue her, bails her out of jail, and gives her money, she tells him
that she regards his concern for her an infantile gesture, a contemptible act.
Indeed, she does not even think enough of him to shoot him, something she
has done not only to her husband but, by this time, to another lover (172–
73). That Lucien becomes here a silly figure is important. Chester Pomeroy
and Patrick Fitzpatrick lose their loves, cling to their own romantic codes,
and face bleak, pointless futures. Nicholas Payne loses Ann without losing
momentum. Lucien, on the other hand, simply cannot maintain the necessary spirit of high romance. He can become neither a melancholy drinker
nor a glorious Jesse James in the romanticized West of his mind. At one
point, he even admits he is "glad he never faced the frontier" (53).

When Emily exits the novel, she appears to take with her McGuane's
fascination with outlawry, seen especially in the screenplays. Her criminal
nature is accentuated when outside lights break through the blinds and
cover her body with stripes (171), suggesting a convict's clothing. Ultimately, as Emily's plane enters the Montana night, Lucien cannot discrimi-
nate between its lights and the stars (173). Outlawry, then, seems banished
to the realm of the mythic nineteenth-century West, the transcendent world
of Pegasus and Pecos Bill. It is, as Emily fears, the end of the romanticized
life (172).

Indeed, the West in *Something to Be Desired* is, on the one hand, mostly
beautiful scenery serving as a backdrop for "coyotes, schemers, and venture
capitalists" (123). W. T. Austinberry, Emily's hired hand, is hardly a cowboy. He cannot chase cattle on horseback over rough ground (39) and cannot sexually satisfy Emily. In fact, this lonesome cowboy is that ultimate of
macho failures, the premature ejaculator (169). At one point, Lucien thinks
of the Indians, whose presence in the contemporary West is a mere echo:
"How could a country produce orators for thousands of years, then a hundred years of yep and nope?" (122). Without Indians or glorious cowboys,

there seems to be no foundation, no strong sense of real myth to build on. Only old limping ranch hands serve as reminders of better days (125). The West is a pale imitation of its imagined self. Lucien, like all contemporary westerners, is a human being without obvious and clear meaning. He seems quite lost, belonging neither in town nor in the mountains (77). He knows he must restore some sort of center to his life (161) and begins to understand that life is not a system into which he moves but a reality he must create for himself. Such a task is difficult, and Lucien is just beginning to realize the exact nature of that difficulty.

On the other hand, the West remains for Lucien a kind of truncated new Eden: "The stream wound through brush in open country. There were antelope off near the limits of visibility, and rising and settling clouds of blackbirds. The pools were sandy and the trout hovered in small schools like fish in the ocean" (157). Such stretches of open country are reminiscent of the infinite possibility of the frontier West and provide Lucien with the tranquility he needs for self-reflection and restoration. Ever since he was a boy, he has been escaping to the hills. It is from *being* back in Montana that he begins again to sense the self he can be. But because this is the twentieth-century West, such stretches of open country exist side by side with the not-necessarily-glorious developments of free enterprise. And Lucien, because he executes a glorious feat, a feat McGuane refers to as "this wonderfully American crackpot piece of venture capitalism,"[4] becomes heir to the best of both centuries.

Once he owns Emily's ranch and develops the health spa, Lucien becomes rich. He has risked much in unconventional ways and—new for a McGuane protagonist—gained that which is admired by conventional society. He becomes not only a man of property but, even more surprisingly, a man of respectability. Lucien, once his new wealth requires him to reinstate a semblance of order in his life, begins to want to think of himself as a working man with a family to support. He is, despite his sexual adventuring, McGuane's most respectable and responsible protagonist since James Quinn in *The Sporting Club*. Lucien is an effective spa manager. He worries about his responsibilities, his guests, and—nearly unbelievable for a McGuane protagonist—his community. We see him discharge the endless tasks of his average day and realize Lucien Taylor is a man who gets things done (157). McGuane, however, is careful that we understand Lucien is not exactly a conventional representative of crass contemporary society. Getting rich only for the sake of getting rich was never Lucien's goal; he had no idea he was going to become extremely wealthy, and becoming even richer does not really interest him (142).

The important point is that Lucien, like his father before him, misses his son (50). McGuane explains, "Lucien had looked at his life and was ready for a new one" (57). This is the second time he wants a new life; that was the excuse he used to leave his family in the first place. But this time we understand that the desire is deeper and more purposeful. McGuane is clear here: Lucien asks Suzanne and James back with "no hint of insincerity" (81). When Lucien's family finally comes within his reach—they come to the ranch for a visit—McGuane explains that Lucien "had never been so in love in his life" (94). Here Lucien epitomizes the driving force behind the westering impulse. Fundamentally, he desires fulfillment that transcends the wealth the sulfur spring has brought him. That the ranch is a successful investment is not enough. He wants a home; he wants to bring order to the chaos of his life. He develops a new resolve and acts to effect the fulfillment he seeks.

The novel's major glimmer of hope for fulfillment in the contemporary West derives from Lucien's relationship with his son. Lucien first attempts to reach James through his own interests. The telling scene occurs when Lucien takes James out to band some hawks. On their way, James has the sensation that his father is going to kidnap him and never let him go (120). Although the thought is not in Lucien's mind, it deliberately evokes the novel's beginning, reminding us that for both fathers, the ultimate sense of well-being rests in their being in possession of their sons.

As they bait the hawk trap with a live barn pigeon, Lucien remembers a boyhood experience of killing an antelope. An old and almost lame cowboy came along and helped him pack the meat out; Lucien, however, told everybody his absent father was the one who helped him (122). Lucien wonders what evoked this memory, but we can credit him with the deep realization that he does not want his son to grow up without a father.

When the hawk strikes the pigeon, James screams and crawls off (124). As Lucien bands the hawk, James shakes. While Lucien admires the hawk, the boy's natural inclination is to cradle the dead pigeon; he manifests a sense of compassion his father naturally lacks. The violent world of nature is anathema to James. Again McGuane is clear: Lucien "rather liked having a boy who was [timid]" (125). Lucien can appreciate the sense that as a strong man he is needed here, and at the same time can see that his son is made of more delicate and sensitive stuff than himself. Still, McGuane is not going to let the situation dissolve in sentimentality: later James explains that killing pigeons is how hawks have to live (130). But the fact remains that James was terrified by the killing; his explanation is not so much an emulation of his father's more hard-boiled ways as an acceptance of them as his father's ways. James, then, is actually reaching toward a relationship with his father.

What is important is that Lucien is attempting to reestablish his family because doing so would benefit all of them, not just him alone. It is one of the few non-self-consumed acts committed by a McGuane protagonist. Lucien would like not to see his child become a "hostage to oblivion" (126) and wonders how he could have left him unguarded (148). His reward is that James begins to no longer fear his father—a major step toward maturity, given that Lucien always feared his own father (173).

McGuane himself sees *Something to Be Desired* as a positive novel. He explains that "through the magical medium of his own child, [Lucien] suddenly steps away from his own ego and sees in fact there is something better out there, and that's the world and the people in it."[5] McGuane does not, however, let his protagonist achieve redemption in any facile way. Lucien must understand that stable family life in the contemporary West is something he must earn. Suzanne is not a flat character occupying space in the novel just to accommodate Lucien and welcome the sadder-but-wiser protagonist back into her arms. In McGuane's hands she is skeptical and tough. In explaining to Lucien why she is hesitant to return to him, she tells him the truth about himself (and, by association, we understand the truth about many of McGuane's protagonists): "No more fucking you, and here's why: it encourages all your sloppy sentimentality and your no-shows and your desertions and your treatment of people who love you as if they were so many pocket mirrors for you to see if you're aging or what kind of day you're having or how deep and creative you are or how effective and memorable your personal philosophy is or whether you might not start going back to church or how many months it was since your last complete physical or whether you ought to give up after-dinner drinks" (154). She is not going to be a supporting player in Lucien's scenario about how Lucien became a responsible adult in the contemporary West. Lucien is going to have to understand her on her own terms as an independent and worthy person.

Before the novel's end, Suzanne no longer thinks of Lucien as a totally selfish person, and even though she admits to loving him (165), she is not sure if she is ready to trust him (173). As she and James drive away from the ranch, McGuane tells us that "Suzanne kept her eye on the road" (173). She clearly is charting her own course, one that takes her directly away from Lucien. We can hope that a fulfilling union is possible and that McGuane is right when he says his protagonist is a changed man, but we cannot know for certain. The ending in itself, of course, is not important. What is important is that McGuane, at this stage in his career, in opening Lucien Taylor's eyes to the possibilities of a life shared with other people, has identified the course for individual fulfillment in spite of the fractured nature of life in the contemporary West. In this instance, Lucien is, as another denotation of his name indicates, a bringer of light.

What Lucien essentially discovers is that it is not all right to be the father his own father was. Experiencing high romance—sexual or otherwise—and battling with one's spouse do not constitute the fully actualized life. Lucien begins to understand that ultimately much of what his life means—to him or anyone else—depends on the meaning defined by his own actions and goals. Indeed, Lucien develops a sense of high romance about venture capitalism, heretofore an unlikely source for adventure in McGuane's work. The romance he develops, of course, is not exactly frontier romance in the sense of Pecos Bill or Jesse James. McGuane has simply rechanneled his energy and redefined the concept to fit his own situation. He has developed an island of professional skill, and he intensely seeks to create the necessary family continuity to achieve meaning and a fulfilling life in the twentieth-century West. That such normal activities can seem romantic to Lucien is the result of his interpretation of their worth. In essence, Lucien has developed his own renewing ritual by infusing twentieth-century reality with the spirit of the nineteenth-century concept of infinite possibility.

Lucien has not completely surrendered his notion of having things both ways—the romance of the stable home from which to confront the chaos of the nineteenth-century frontier and the high-rolling economic fulfillment of the twentieth. He would prefer not to accept full responsibility for the creation of his own life. It is his sexuality, for instance, not his own self-absorption, that so often gets him into trouble. It was not his idea to have sex with his friend Dee in the bank foyer or to enjoy fellatio with Freddy, a nanny who visits the spa. All this is going on, of course, while the real Lucien decides that it is Suzanne he really loves and wants to spend his life with. Love for Lucien is a highly idealized concept, one that transcends his natural sexual urges. Even though he has spent a winter engaging in indiscriminate sex all around Deadrock, he becomes alarmed when Suzanne speaks of her own sex life as "fuck[ing]" (154). He wants an idealized woman for his romantic notion of a self-contained, sustained family on the contemporary frontier. Indeed, such an actualized life is more to the point than his sense of himself as Emily's rescuing hero. Emily has never needed a savior, and neither, ultimately, does Suzanne.

In this regard, if any character in the novel can teach Lucien what real—as opposed to idealized—women are like, it is Dee, a local woman who is undergoing marital turbulence. Her relationship with her husband,

Gale, a seamless-gutter contractor, is a foil for the Lucien-Suzanne marriage. Dee really is justified in being unhappy. Gale is a hapless businessman who reacts to his wife's infidelity by "blackmailing" Lucien into purchasing seamless gutters for the spa. In the beginning Lucien sees her as just another episode in his current sexual frenzy. Dee, however, is not experienced at infidelity and springs to a life of her own by announcing that being with Lucien makes her feel like a "sewer" (60).

Although Dee and Lucien continue their sexual relationship, they do at least once meet for dinner and dancing without sex. Lucien begins to "like her" (97), to think of her as a friend. In the end Dee leaves Gale, whom she has taken to calling "Shit-for-brains" (159). In essence, Dee is a less dramatic version of the Lucien character. The problem with her marriage is that she wants "to be somebody and [Gale] wants to be nobody" (159). She, however, does not go off wildly in search of high adventure; she leaves town instead to learn the florist business from her sister. The friendship she shares with Lucien is the only unromanticized relationship Lucien has with a woman; it is Dee who sees him through his crack-up (124, 159). What Lucien and Dee have shared is vulnerability. There is a lesson here of which Lucien is only dimly aware at the novel's end. Sincere affection—something he never really held for Suzanne during their marriage—often manifests itself when people simply learn to understand and appreciate each other; the unglamorized presence of a friend can provide the strength to see one through the difficult times. For Lucien, then, this presence takes the form of wanting to gather his family around him to become a unit within which he can function and from which he can derive the strength to live. Suzanne cannot yet decide to stay with Lucien and re-form the family unit, for she cannot be sure Lucien will understand his responsibility to that unit. As the novel ends, he has transferred his notions of romantic adventure to the idea of wife and son, but he has yet to demonstrate commitment.

At this point in the McGuane canon, his protagonist has progressed from a self-absorbed resolve for fulfillment through the high adventure of discord and outlawry to a self-sustaining resolve to settle into a stable family life that rises above personal chaos. Perhaps because so much of the chaos is self-generated and not the result of American crassness, Lucien is the first protagonist since Quinn to opt for such obviously conventional stability. Lucien also clearly points up the need for McGuane's protagonists to re-create their own family units because, for whatever reason, the parents are absent. They are dead, or their systems of values are useless to the worlds the protagonists find themselves in. Discord and outlandish behavior are not enough; the protagonists must invent their own despair-curing islands. In this way they

confront twentieth-century life armed with a sense of nineteenth-century infinite possibility. A subtle hint that this approach provides the greatest
chance for fulfillment is evident when Suzanne takes James to see the wild
mustangs on the Wind River Range and the Red Desert (173)—the actual
remaining vestiges of the West that James has previously only read about
(157). Even though he may well spend his life in an eastern city, James will
confront the world from within the legacy of infinite possibility. He will be a
gentler and more sensitive version of his father, but he will embody that aspect of the spirit of the nineteenth-century West which leads most produc-
tively to individual fulfillment. Whatever their circumstances, McGuane
protagonists persevere most successfully when they never lose sight of the
possibilities for renewal embodied in such spirit.

Chapter Nine

To Skin a Cat: Something Old, Something New

Overview

Thomas McGuane recognizes *To Skin a Cat* as the culmination of a conscious effort to broaden the range of his creative skills: "I had been admiring short stories for a long time, and, basically, I wanted to understand how they are written." As part of his preparation, he read all 13 volumes of Chekhov's short fiction. He remarks, "Reading Chekhov is an education. It has greater importance than three years at Yale." Chekhov, he thinks, is a great example of the power-to-weight ratio. As additional analogues he cites naval architects, whose goal is hull structures manifesting the greatest strength with the greatest lightness, and the English, who build a 16-gauge shotgun that weighs five pounds. "I have this aesthetic notion that economy of means is always the thing," McGuane explains.

Once into this new adventure, McGuane discovered that a single story took as long as two months to write and the collection—all but two of the stories were new—nearly three years. Although most major journals did not review the book, the critical response in newspapers across America was positive. Such acclaim, however, has not impelled McGuane to attempt another collection. He is essentially a novelist, and a practical one at that: "I would love to be the next great short story writer, but something is lost if you are doing something that is not read. Short stories are basically read only by other short story writers. We like to imagine that artists exist in an art for art's sake vacuum, but they really don't. They live in the human universe."

Critical Reception

To Skin a Cat was reviewed in only one major periodical, the *New York Times Book Review*. Elizabeth Tallent's essay is positive in tone and mostly concerned with analyzing and explaining McGuane's history. She compares his dialogue with Hemingway's—by now an almost-expected point—but also cites Tim O'Brien and Flannery O'Connor as fellow practitioners of the "grim waywardness of reality."[1] She sees "Like a Leaf" and "To Skin a Cat" as too bleak, repelling the reader at the times when they do not enthrall. Such a remark is almost praise considering that the pictures of women in these two stories could be interpreted as sexist and abusive in the extreme. Essentially, Tallent feels that McGuane's people are alone in the world and that readers must "confront the extent and intensity of that aloneness" (14). In a sidebar, McGuane is quoted from a telephone interview: "I'm interested in writing about what used to be called 'fatal attractions'—about people who seem drawn to bad ideas. It's not that I think fatal attraction is a good thing, though" (13). He appears eager to correct those who insist on finding the philosophy of Thomas McGuane the person to be one and the same with that of the characters he creates. Often a target for angry (and arguably righteously so, at times) feminists, McGuane felt quite complimented by Tallent's piece: "I was really pleased to have a good woman writer review my work, and I was incredibly flattered when she thought I had written a good book."

A Reading

To Skin a Cat calls forth various literary presences. A number of the stories are set in Faulkner country, at least one displaying the humor of the sly southwestern good old boy. Hemingway's grim visage remains stalwart beneath the surface of stories dealing with initiation and death. And while echoes of the younger, more satirical McGuane appear in numerous pieces concerned with financial transactions of one kind or another, McGuane's concern for the decline of the nineteenth-century West is evident throughout. In addition, McGuane himself appears to be assaying a new topic in stories centering on midlife crises, and in one story he appears to be experimenting with dreams.

The dream story, "Like a Leaf," seems on first reading to be the most troubling of the collection. Set in Deadrock, it concerns a narrator whose wife has recently died and a love affair he has with a desirable woman who lives across the street. The woman ultimately seduces the narrator, who after years of marital fidelity comes to the affair with virginal innocence. Previously, the woman had been entertaining Deke Patwell while Deke's wife has been out of town. McGuane's concern for the decline of the West is readily visible here. Patwell, representative of the crass new West in *Nobody's Angel*, is perceived by the narrator as "a crude foreigner or a gaucho."[2] To a solid

old-timer ("one of this area's better cattlemen" [40]) like the narrator,
Patwell is an obnoxious interloper. The truth is that the narrator is not
equipped to function in the new West. He represents the everyday, decent
Montana resident who can neither understand nor tolerate the new crassness. When this new and exciting woman rapes him, he thinks of his deceased and faithful wife and cries.

The action becomes surreal when the narrator introduces the woman to
his friend, a guard at the prison. One thing leads to another, and we realize
the woman is an out-of-control nymphomaniac who eventually has sex with
all the inmates. Such an extremely macho depiction of woman has been absent in McGuane's work since *The Bushwhacked Piano*. The woman appears
unredeemably one-dimensional and the author slightly less insensitive than
Attila the Hun—until, that is, we look more closely. The key appears early
in the story when the narrator mentions that he is seeing a psychiatrist and
says that when he loses control of his life, he plans to smoke opium: "Doc
and I agree on one thing: it's all in your head. . . . Because we believe it's all
in your head, we believe in immortality. . . . Without [immortality] I don't
get to see my wife again. . . . When Doc and I grow old and the end is in
sight, we're going to become addicted to opium. If we get our timing
wrong, we'll cure ourselves with aspirin" (42–43).

From then on, the story appears to be progressing as a realistic narrative,
but slowly—as in a dream—reality begins to unravel. The narrator mis-
judges his timing. He courts the woman in conventional fashion, being nicer
than Patwell to her, but she does not respond according to conventional expectations. He is unprepared for rape, having instead prepared for immortality by reading Ralph Waldo Emerson, who only here and there, and
almost grudgingly, acknowledges the presence of potential evil in
experience.

In a self-reliant manner Emerson would approve of, the narrator seeks to
free himself from the roller-coaster disintegration of his own dream. He says
good-bye to Doc and announces, "I'm going it alone" (50). But in truth he
buries himself more deeply in his own head. After the prison episode, he es-
corts the nymphomaniac out to the river and shoots her. The language here
is revealing: "The little homewrecker kneels at the end of the sandbar and
washes herself over and over. When I am certain she feels absolutely clean, I
let her have it" (55). The question then becomes, What home has she
wrecked? On two levels the home is the narrator's. Once he finds that this
new woman is not conventionally sweet and nice, he can see her only as
someone who has come between himself and his dead wife. She also repre-

sents the rapine new West that maintains no respect for the old-timer's sense of decency.

Once he has struck this blow for the past, the narrator says, "We never did need the social whirl. . . . There for a while it looked like the end" (55). The "we" here is the narrator, his wife, and the West of their youth. Since it did look like the end for a while, the narrator has crawled inside his own dream, seemingly oblivious to the new West personified in Patwell and the nymphomaniac.

"Dogs" and "Rescue" depict midlife protagonists fighting the finality of aging with all the reckless abandon of McGuane's youthful protagonists warring against conventionality. Like the earlier protagonists, they are not always sympathetic or likable. Fifty-one-year-old Howie Reed, in "Dogs," can't stop time, and so he resorts to mild hysteria. Shortly after he undergoes a face-lift, his wife leaves him. Then, like a frontier outlaw, he begins stealing dogs. Even though he is a successful insurance agent who has done everything right, he frantically quests for his own sense of freedom by staging a head-on assault against Deadrock society. At a party given by a new physician, whose dog he has already stolen, Howie becomes immoderately offensive. In some of McGuane's best comic writing since *Bushwhacked Piano*, Howie, among other thrusts, insults the food and the host's wife, and in crowning achievement, greets a pregnant woman with "I see you've been fucking" (62).

Howie's high jinks are played off against the pack instinct of the community. The socially conforming locals are outraged. Even though Howie has been a friend to everyone, they will not tolerate his assault on propriety. The prevailing sentiment is "Let's kill Howie" (63). What they don't understand is that Howie has found his Horatio Alger–like achievements (62) to be lifeless. He is too successful; his future is too assured. There are no new discoveries in the new West: "Now everything seemed so final" (61). The point here is the same as it is for McGuane's youthful protagonists. Howie has been seeking to renew his life by creating his own frontier: "I felt like Balboa when he saw the Pacific. I'd never known anything like it" (64).

In "Rescue" Albert Buckland simply cannot tolerate his life any longer and attempts to do just that: buck the land. After taking refuge in alcohol—certainly not a new method for survival in a one-horse town—he achieves a new pinnacle of disgrace by forcing his sexual attentions on a CPR dummy in front of his fellow credit-union directors and a well-meaning but ineffectual CPR instructor. McGuane adroitly paints Buckland's audience: the directors display all the go-along and get-along verve of the cattlemen's association in *Tom Horn*, and the instructor is overly zealous and condescending.

Once again we have a protagonist who cannot abide the people he must live around or what he has made of his life. Albert has already violated a basic tenet of the community: he has never held a job. Born wealthy, his only achievement is as an elk hunter (88). His wife, a middle class woman in a traditional small town, worries mostly about appearances and keeping her rugs clean. When she hears of Albert's indiscretion, she banishes him from their home. Albert refers to himself as "the real Duke of Athole ["asshole" with a lisp, we can assume]" (93), suggesting that he knows he is not on his best behavior, but the forces that drive him will not permit him to stop.

The narrator, a cattle trader, tries to save Albert from himself by being friend enough to meet him at a local restaurant. When Albert creates a scene, the narrator concludes the interview, wanting Albert beaten for discourtesy. Albert appears to have eliminated all his options in the community, but even his messy behavior in the restaurant serves his purpose because "people looked" (93). Notice me, he seems to be saying, and commits the eternal sin of wanting to rage against the dying of the day. When he winds up in the hospital after a commode-hugging drunk, his estranged wife feels compelled—by convention, no doubt—to take him back within the security of the life against which he raged. And so he becomes a helpless prisoner of stability. Albert Buckland looms as a Nicholas Payne gone wrong, a Vernor Stanton with no concrete concept such as the Centennial Club to rage against, and in the end can only destroy himself. Convention, it seems, will not be bucked.

The need for purpose at midlife and the frontierless modern West come together in "The Road Atlas." Bill Berryhill (the name suggests that this protagonist is a man of nature; it also echoes the title of the old song "Blueberry Hill," and *blue* is an accurate word for the malaise Bill finds himself in) shares his car, its inside resembling a disaster area, with his collie Elaine. Although he appears to be a shaggy frontiersman in the clean-cut new West, Bill and his brothers own a portfolio of investments about which his brothers are constantly calling meetings. But Bill is not a team player, and to further exacerbate the situation, he is tired of business slang and his MBA-holding brothers, who wield such slang in pursuit of largess. He wonders why his brothers "can't be happy in an ordinary way" (144). Bill feels a "mandate for greater meaning" (146), whereas his brothers just want more of what they have. Brother John tells him, "Your search for meaning is a bore" (147). The frontier where Bill can find himself is no longer there. If new settlements are to be made, they will be staked out in portfolios.

Bill's problem is that his education—he reads the quarterlies—and his old-fashioned sense of values combine to render him superfluous. He loves Elizabeth, his frequent lunch companion, but he sleeps with Karen. Karen is a local salesclerk who signs phony signatures to gift-shop pottery. The purity of his relationship with Elizabeth is demonstrated by her unwillingness to sleep with him, and in remorse about Karen, Bill hopes he develops venereal disease. He appears not to know who he is. He wants something pure; at the same time, he wants sex. And he does not like life or himself very much.

The story takes its title from a vacation that Bill and Elizabeth plan. It starts small—Monticello, the home of Thomas Jefferson, the American president who solidified the potential of the frontier when he engineered the Louisiana Purchase—and keeps burgeoning until they plan to include the Alamo and Bunker Hill—places where human beings distinguished themselves over ideals that transcend portfolios. Slowly Bill becomes timid. Eventually, the plan is for Liz to go alone—Bill just cannot bring himself to leave his ranch.

Bill's inability to leave stems partly from concern over the kinds of transactions his brothers might concoct in his absence but more importantly from knowledge that his ranch provides him with the entirety of his self-concept. Go or stay, Bill is not happy. Caught in a maze of his own inaction, he simply cannot decide, cannot come to concrete terms with himself: "I feel something is passing me up and I don't know what it is. . . . I see my vital interests drifting into growth areas. It's platitudinous. I wish I could see myself as subsisting . . . tied to the land or some God damn thing" (143).

McGuane's midlife protagonists are reminiscent of the young McGuane protagonists. All quest to elude the finality of existence. While the young try not to settle down, the old try not to admit they have settled. Whatever their lives have come to, they cannot accept the outcome as fulfillment. They cannot recognize themselves for who they are but instead persist in seeing life as "cloudiness and an irresolute foreground" (143). In a West part old, part new, part myth, and part undistinguished conventionality, they simply do not know how to proceed.

The characters in the stories concerned with financial transactions bring to mind the upper-middle-class pretentious so deftly satirized in *The Sporting Club* and *The Bushwhacked Piano*. Like the club members and the Fitzgeralds, McGuane's people here are unabashedly self-absorbed. They are concerned mostly with not being hampered, with being allowed to do exactly as they please. They do not rage against an established order; rather, they acquire their values entirely from it. They are establishment-centered, upwardly mobile Americans who expect to win because they know how to comply with rules they have never questioned.

"The Millionaire" concerns the predicaments of Jack and Betty, whose empty marriage began with a courtship resembling a Hollywood movie. Their life has resulted in all the tangibles of the American dream, except that their 15-year-old daughter, Iris, is pregnant. This situation so upsets the parents that they have taken a summer house 100 miles from their normal environs in order to barter the illegitimate child to a childless judge from whom Jack needs a decision to save his factory. Unwed pregnancies and under-the-table dealing do not confirm the myth of happiness inherent in the American dream, and Jack and Betty hope that by transacting such business out of town, they can pretend it never happened.

As we wait for the baby to be born, McGuane deftly slashes away the veneer of upper-middle-class life. The summer home is on a body of water known as Lake Polliwog, indicating the small, unrealized nature of the individuals involved. Betty is unhappy because the lake does not have the welcoming smell of the ocean "or so much as a single Pocahontas or other legendary figure connected with it" (10). Ordinary reality is not enough for her; everything must somehow be clean, as in a 1940s Hollywood movie. For instance, their dog, Brucie, had to be put to sleep because he never "learned to potty outside" (7). Since reality is simply too harsh and too mundane a proposition, Betty drinks in the daytime to create "an atmosphere of emergency" (15). The men in the story uphold the American myth of getting ahead: Jack sees himself as "a red-blooded American with his own business" (11); the doctor, an upbeat Scandinavian, appears like "the grand prize on a quiz show" (8) and arrives direct from the golf course, still in his spikes; Judge Anse wants Iris's baby because he cannot adopt a Caucasian baby through legal channels, and he must have an heir to whom he can leave his money—the results of his devotion to the system.

These people are firmly ensconced in upper-middle-class values. They believe life must work out in a nice way, the way traditional expectations have led them to believe it's supposed to. But they discover that reality has other plans. As they await the arrival of the baby, Jack expresses the shock of recognition: "I'm about to become a grandfather. . . . This means we're starting to die. That jackass doctor upstairs is shoving us into history" (20). Life here is simply not all that Jack assumed it would be. He is nothing special; he is a conventional man living a normal life span. When Judge Anse remarks that considering he is about to become a "father," he doesn't feel as young as he should, Jack responds to the self-absorbed, supercilious statement with the suggestion that he try Grecian Formula Nine. The remark offends the judge, but more importantly it signals the complete artificiality of this upper-middle-class world in which people adhere to convention and seemingly lack the essential human courage to deal with adversity. At one point Betty moans, "Whatever happened to our luck?" (16) as if luck, rather than courage and stamina, were the only means of achievement and survival.

If there is a ray of hope in the story, it exists solely in Iris. Her name denotes the hardiness of a perennial plant. She is the only one who seems to have a vision beyond the frustrations of the current situation. She takes comfort in the strangeness of pregnancy. Though she is the person the adults have to consider, she is clearly not a part of their concerns. Accepting her lonely plight, she dares to be complacent as their world becomes turbulent. She will not—as her parents are doing—prepare to pretend that her pregnancy and the resulting child never happened. When she bolts the house just before the birth, she is trying to give the baby a fresh start, trying not to bring it into the world of her parents.

As her name would indicate, Iris appears to be the only natural "thing" in the story. She plays with a Swiss army knife like any 15-year-old child. She knows she will survive the birth and go on. The pregnancy is not the end of her life; it is just something that happened to her. The final image is of Iris, happy with the child in her arms and totally oblivious to the idea that the child was born a millionaire. She is attuned to the natural world; she transcends the conventional concerns of her parents' world. McGuane, however, reserves the last word for himself: he does not disclose the sex of the baby, as if to say that in the conventional world, it is more important for the judge to have someone to leave his money to than it is for the child to possess an individual identity. Indeed, the baby is valuable not really for itself alone—except possibly to Iris, who is probably too young to fully understand the meaning of motherhood—but for the opportunities it provides the other characters, suggesting that barter may be more important than life itself in contemporary America.

The last thing Barry Seitz in "A Man in Louisiana" wants is an individual identity. Concerned foremost with his own success, he is the perfect corporate yuppie: "At thirty, a backward move could be a menace to his whole life. . . . The future was an unbroken sheen to Barry, requiring only irreversible solvency" (26). Seitz hates his boss but is willing to devote minute attention to a discussion of his boss's daughter's braces. When the boss sends him into the wilds of Mississippi to purchase a superior hunting dog, Seitz warms quickly to the task because the assignment will prove he is a "can-do guy" (34) and will thus ensure a secure future for him.

Life in rural Mississippi first scares and then charms Seitz, however, and he begins to discover the emptiness of his goals when he meets Jimmy F. Tippett, the owner of Bandit the wonder dog. Tippett is unpretentious and unambitious. The dog, too, touches a chord deeply within Seitz, who begins to sense that there is more to life than he has dreamed of: "He was entirely in the world of Tippett, feeling the senselessness of trading the money for Bandit. . . . Now he had gone over to the other side" (32). He longs to be a part of this world. He orders "S'em up" just like the locals and decides to take Bandit for a run.

When the dog runs off on him, Seitz is first panic-stricken but slowly begins to feel "glumly merry and irresponsible" (35). Beginning to suspect a swindle, he returns to Tippett. The dog's muffled bark from behind Tippett's door telegraphs the message of new life to Seitz: he realizes the dog does not want to go with him, and he is immediately at peace. He shares a drink and a laugh with Tippett "as equals" (36). He thinks of "how a dog could run so far that . . . he never came back" (36), and we understand that Barry Seitz will never return to his old life.

This upwardly mobile yuppie appears to have tapped into a sort of cosmic sensibility that transcends conventional achievement. But the final irony here belongs to McGuane. Seitz, in having gone from playing by corporate rules to playing by those of rural Mississippi, has really only traded one set of rules for another. The first Mississippi rule that Seitz should have learned is that whistle-trained dogs do not obey verbal commands. McGuane—in a touch worthy of William Faulkner's *The Hamlet*—appears to be having his own little joke on his readers, since no direct mention is made of how the dog has actually been trained. That the dog *is* trained is reiterated throughout the story, but the whistle appears only once, hanging from Tippett's neck when we first see him (30).

Dean Robinson, in "Partners," discovers that success can come from changing the corporate rules to fit himself. Robinson has just achieved the status of partner in one of the best law firms in Billings. While the idea of a corporate ladder existing in Billings, Montana, may be somewhat ironic to coastal readers, the law partners themselves believe in their system religiously. When Edward Hooper, one of the senior partners, undertakes to school Dean in the strict code of behavior required for continued achievement, Dean has an uneasy feeling that his life will be permanently impaired.

His life begins to unravel when he is invited to dine with the firm's top client and discovers that the man's wife is one of his old girlfriends. With all the aplomb of Nicholas Payne, Dean ignores the client and makes sexual advances toward his wife. The senior partners are aghast, the work atmosphere becomes chilly, and Dean feels his career will soon be over.

Not wanting to confine himself to the restrictions of corporate success, Dean begins a career of self-destruction. He tells off Hooper and takes the client's wife on a long drive out of town, only to discover that they are simply "good friends" (128). But it is too late. When they return to the woman's home, the client is outraged, and in the ensuing rash of violence all three wind up in the hospital. But the important thing is that Dean stood up to the beating and got in the last lick when he forced an automobile crash. In daring to go where no lawyer has gone before—that is, in standing up to a client—Dean wins a new respect at the office. He lives now in the quickening "rarity of daily life" (131). That which he thought would free him from corporate success has now made him a hero and solidified his place in the firm.

The story ends with the client requesting that Dean replace Hooper as his lawyer. The rebel-made-hero must now resign himself to a life of "solitude and bitter glory" (135). When one dares to live outside the system, one becomes the new version of a Montana mountain man: the orneriest guy at the office. Dean Robinson seems the best man the contemporary West can offer. The use of the word *bitter* here seems to mock the town, the profession, and the entire concept of frontier yuppiedom. Whereas young rebels like Nicholas Payne were "at large," posing at least in their immediate elders' eyes serious threats to the system, Dean's "glory" will be limited to country-club gossip. He need not commit another bizarre act; his reputation as a man to be reckoned with in the rural upwardly mobile society is ensured, whether he likes it or not.

An obsession with upward mobility on the contemporary frontier destroys the marriage of David and Rita in "Little Extras." The story begins with the newlyweds living an austere but happy existence in a trailer at Rita's father's ranch. David is the essential rustic: handsome, simple, hardworking, and muscle-bound. Rita is demure, sweet, cute—and ambitious. And there's the rub. Her insistence that they own their own house—specifically, the one recently vacated on the death of Mr. Penniman, the grocer—leads them on an adventure that shatters their union and leaves David, the pure simpleton, with no West to be pure and simple in.

The young couple purchase the Penniman house, thinking they are also purchasing the furniture. Mrs. Callahan, the grocer's daughter, however, has the right to a day in the house to gather keepsakes. The discovery that "keepsakes," in this case, turn out to be all of the old man's furniture and possessions destroys Rita's hopes for a rosy future. Undaunted, the couple attend Mrs. Callahan's rodeo party in an attempt to achieve a separate peace.

McGuane is at his satirical best here. The party echoes the disintegration of the Centennial Club. The greatest concern is whether the chili will be satisfactory. Outside it rains. Water may be cleansing, but the only thing washed away here is the veneer of respectability. The crowd becomes more drunken, the innuendos bolder, and Mrs. Callahan throws chili at a particularly sarcastic guest. While "Gary Owen," General George Armstrong Custer's theme song, plays in the background, Rita demolishes the gathering by physically engaging Mrs. Callahan and leaving her in a neck brace. A legal fight ensues, which requires the hiring of lawyer Neville, a notorious local ladies' man.

David's, not Custer's, last stand, however, is imminent. Since David has no notion of the female orgasm, Rita is easily seduced by Neville and before long is devoting herself entirely to his upper-crusty pursuits of gambling and horseback riding. Making a niche for oneself in the old West was never like this. David realizes he no longer has a place in Rita's life, and Rita dismisses him because he "has no love of the struggle" (114), the phrase she uses to refer to her life of questing for justice, which includes wanting above all else a nice home and a microwave.

Once the town is certain Rita has left David, Mrs. Callahan returns the furniture. The connections here are deft, ironic, and amusing. She tells David that she wanted something to remember her father by. We understand that David is that something. Mrs. Callahan is alone, the father was alone, and David is alone. David is a walking memory of her father: a lone man living in her father's house. He becomes the new version of the lone frontiersman in the contemporary West: his options are "computer technician school and the Navy recruiter" (117).

McGuane's least likable protagonist, Bobby Decatur, appears in "To Skin a Cat," published in *TriQuarterly* in 1981, after *Panama* and before *Nobody's Angel*. The story seems to have come from that more fatalistic time in McGuane's life. Its tone is one of hopelessness and self-destruction.

Decatur is a 30-year-old rich brat who, like so many of McGuane's men, "helplessly exudes privilege" (163). The story reads much like a movie treatment; indeed, the plot itself is an absurdist twist on the conventional Hollywood formula of boy meets girl, boy gets girl, boy loses girl, boy gets girl back. All is true here except the fourth ingredient; in "To Skin a Cat," boy gets what he deserves.

Ostensibly in London to sell a falcon, American westerner Bobby meets Marianne, an American abroad visiting her fiancé. Through outlandish boyish charm, Bobby seduces Marianne away from her boyfriend, and they eventually settle in San Francisco. Bobby does not have to work; his income comes from the original family ranch in Deadrock, a homestead he is only nominally in charge of. (In the *TriQuarterly* version, Bobby comes from Jackson Hole, Wyoming, suggesting that McGuane had not yet settled on Deadrock as his Yoknapatawpha.) Unfortunately for Marianne, the major obsession of Bobby's life is to become a pimp. Because she loves him, she willingly consents to be part of his fantasy, and through a series of misadventures, she becomes lost to "the life." At first Bobby is cute and brash; then he becomes pointless and reprehensible until, finally, Marianne plunges a knife into his neck. Bobby falls dead and no one cares, not even the policeman who must dispose of the remains.

Besides pimps, Decatur's other passion is for falcons, or in this case, prairie hawks—violent birds that drop from the skies to prey on the weak. Decatur likes pimps because they too "prey on the world" (170). This dropping to prey on, of course, is what Bobby does to Marianne. The earlier version of "To Skin a Cat" makes the point much more bitterly than the book version that everybody falls prey to somebody or something. In the original script, McGuane seems to be giving us his own view of what the country has come to because his characters take pains to point out that everybody "in the world has a pimp."[3] They single out specifically the Bank of America and a famous though unnamed football player promoting his book at B. Dalton's. The player himself is not substance but cliché: "The game has made me a better person. Once I was a follower. Now I am a leader. I am the game and the game is me. My country gave me that game. I stand tall because of it. I understand incentive and seek to share my understanding with you. Nobody wants to be a loser. I'm not a loser. I'm a winner. I owe it all to football" (39). The football player's pimp is the American way of success. "Leader," "winner," "better person," "stand tall"—all represent an inherited and profane value system. The player gives no indication that he has developed any insight into his own situation. He knows he has survived so far because he has played football. His only way to see himself clearly is

through his connection to the game. Because we know that "the book" usually comes out just as any player's career is about over, just before his name
begins to fade, we can wonder if this player is trying to convince himself that
he is a winner and not someone who will become a "loser" once the game no
longer requires his presence. And so the player promotes his book to achieve
one final success, and in so doing, he illustrates that football in America is
not about sportsmanship or individual worth or becoming better people;
rather, it is simply about making money, at bottom simply a heartless business. McGuane's explanation for cutting the football player from the final
version is that the author "stepped out of voice. I don't like that in fiction. I
like fiction to have its world. I don't need to stop and say here's a dope from
the world of football."

Love, too, appears to be about making money in America. (Although we
may interpret their use of the term as meaning "sex," McGuane's characters
use the word *love* to describe their transactions.) One of the story's whores
explains that prostitution is not humiliating "unless you don't get paid"
(204). This character too seems to give no indication of an awareness that
the "game" of prostitution is debasing her, robbing her of any potential self-
worth. Money, then, is the motivating force for Americans, and because
Decatur was born with more than enough money, he must find a goal other
than the accumulation of wealth to fulfill himself. Pimping becomes his last
frontier.

The idea that Bobby is in quest of his last frontier is supported by his respect for the self-reliance of hawks—and by association, pimps—and his remark after a visit to Golden Gate Park. He sees anglers casting into fishless
pools, and pet buffalo—"great mementos grazing in the coastal fog" (182):
"There you have it. The American West. I feel weak all over" (182).
Bobby's own ranch is not enough, and he has westered to San Francisco to
find purposeless anglers and buffalo that do not roam. We are to understand that he fears achievement will elude his grasp when he says, "My life
passed before my eyes, and I concluded . . . that there was not a minute to
be lost. Let's hit the streets" (182). And so he goes about hawking
Marianne.

Prostitution itself is described in terms of profane success. Chino, the
story's real pimp, once read "that more Americans can recognize the
McDonald's hamburger than the national anthem" (203). Chino immediately began to believe that he and McDonald's were in direct competition. A cynical McGuane is dominant in "To Skin a Cat." Eating a meal at
a fast-food restaurant is as much like eating a real meal as having sex with

a prostitute is like experiencing real emotional involvement with a genuine loved one.

During her series of misadventures, Marianne falls under the control of Chino and becomes an almost-priceless commodity: an unwilling whore. Chino does not really want to compete with McDonald's. He wants—in his own spirit of the frontier—to quest beyond offering his customers a meal on a bun. He desires a product for the discerning, a product that will appeal to his client's search for new adventure (199). At one point, Chino appears to be drawing inspiration from watching the classic western *Red River* on television (209–10). The symbolism is plain: the unwilling woman becomes the last frontier, the last great conquest for the last frontiersman. In the process, Marianne becomes a genuine whore and discovers that she has no former self to return to (209–11). Marianne is herself a victim of the need for romantic adventure, of the notion that there is always something more. She has been worried that life is passing her by. She has broken two engagements because she fears marriage would require her to "disappear without a trace" (188). She has been poised for someone like Bobby to escort her to the last frontier.

When Bobby finally rescues her and takes her home, Marianne will not make love with him unless she is paid. Then follows a very ambiguous passage: "And for once in Bobby's life pure desire pours through him like flame" (212). "Pure desire" is the ambiguous phrase here. On the one hand, we can accentuate the "pure" and credit Bobby with experiencing compassion and empathy at the awareness of Marianne's degradation and, finally, loving her for herself alone. If this is true, Bobby's death becomes sad and pointless. On the other hand, if "desire" is the major term, we can understand that Bobby is ready to venture into the last frontier. He remains the selfish brat who began the process of transforming Marianne into a whore; he nearly achieves the goal he set for himself when he hit the streets: like football franchise owners, he now owns his own professional. In this case, his death is the result of his dream of conquering his conception of the last frontier.

McGuane wants us to make no mistake. The idea of infinite possibility embodied in the myth of the frontier West has gone out of control. The story ends as follows: "A stretcher [carrying Bobby's unidentified body] passes covered with a sheet, the anonymous contents of which constitute a valediction to every long walk off every short pier in America" (212). Bobby's life, then, *is* sad and pointless. He has perished in pursuit of an impossible quest, one that, like westering for fulfillment, has always been impossible in its pure form and has required compromise on the part of the quester. What is sad and unforgivable is that Bobby Decatur has destroyed the life of the one person who loves him. Unlike Chester Hunnicutt Pomeroy's Catherine, Marianne appears doomed to the life Bobby chose for her and cannot generate the resolve to escape. McGuane seems to be saying that disaster, though not always this bleak, is inevitable for the westerer. He concludes "To Skin a Cat" with the words of the policeman who has supervised the removal of Bobby's body: "I cannot offer any encouragement that your readers will ever hear the end of this story" (212). Such achievers as Bobby Decatur will continue to fall victim to their own illusions.

Four of the stories display none of the fascination with satirizing transactions. They depict a Hemingway-like initiation—to life, to death. McGuane takes us into the world of men young and old who, finding life more than they are prepared for, have no choice but to respond with grace under pressure.

"A Skirmish" is set in the upper Midwest, territory familiar to McGuane and Hemingway. Because the narrator, a young boy in grade school, probably in the fifties, wears a blue Civil War soldier cap, he must confront the notoriously mean and futureless Emery brothers, who buck convention and dare to wear the gray. The narrator, outnumbered and outsized, endures constant harassment—indeed, even the breaking of his leg—without outwardly wincing. Ultimately, the Emerys jail him in an old piano crate, where they intend to keep him until he repudiates his allegiance to Abraham Lincoln by proclaiming that Lincoln was a coward.

Hovering between "terror and opportunity" (75), the narrator sets fire to the crate and is rescued by the Emerys' out-of-work father—the local odd-job and junk man. What the young man learns inadvertently is class consciousness. Comparing his sons with the narrator, the father says, "They're not like you, are they? . . . You'll always have something you can do" (75). The narrator's presence is as disturbing to the Emerys as theirs is to him. The doomed plight of the Emerys is still not apparent to the boy; nor is the idea of self-reliance, a quality he has continually exhibited. Although the narrator is always frightened of the Emery brothers, he endures the continued hassle without self-pity. He has freed himself from their jail, and more importantly, he has kept to the rigors of his own code of honor and displayed grace under pressure. It doesn't matter that Abraham Lincoln was not cowardly; what matters is that the narrator could not call him a coward without betraying himself.

In "Sportsmen," set in Michigan, the narrator and his friend Jimmy Meade are two 13-year-olds who think of themselves as duck hunters. They are outdoorsmen who thrive on the code of the wilds and circumspectly avoid the local hoods, who do not respect nature and are not compatible with natural life-giving forces. In a freak accident Jimmy breaks his neck and becomes permanently paralyzed. The narrator, in a rush of guilt and bewilderment, leaves town and works in a factory among the restorative forces of good country people. When he returns, he finds Jimmy the companion of the very hoods they tried so hard to avoid. Jimmy even has given up talking in his fascinating lower-Ohio voice and begun to speak like a hood. Afraid but committed, the narrator reclaims his old friend: "What I did was just sit there and tough it out until the room got tense and people just began to pick up and go" (101).

The two of them go to hunt ducks, the narrator ready to shoot and Jimmy strapped to his board and watching. Suddenly they are caught in a snowstorm, the ducks huddling around them like a raft. They are the center of a natural world. They feast on two of the ducks and Jimmy's almost-southern accent returns. When the story concludes on the line "the earth turned clean round again" (103), the meaning of "clean" is clear: nature has cleansed the situation. The relationship is reestablished; their former world has returned. In a world in which life plays dirty tricks, the narrator has learned to live with things he cannot change, to rely on natural forces and endure as best as he can. The skills required for duck hunting provide him with the necessary foundation of confidence against the strange and violent ways of the hoods. He and Jimmy are sportsmen once again.

The other two stories deal with that old Hemingway standby, confronting death. In "Two Hours to Kill"—which appears to be set in Faulkner country—Jack has returned to the old homestead to attend his dead mother's body. He cannot bring himself to face the fact of her death. In fact, he will not view the body until the authorities arrive, and so he takes his horse and his dogs out to hunt quail. Like Nick Adams in Hemingway's "Big Two-hearted River," Jack returns to nature to get over death. Death, however, intrudes when the dogs unnerve Jack by going on point when they mistake gravestones for other dogs on point. The dead, it appears, will triumph.

When the ranch bell tolls, summoning him back to the house because the body tenders have arrived, Jack turns his horse at a full gallop as if attempting to escape time itself. Ultimately, he falls into a ditch he had intended to jump, only to wake up in an ambulance with the corpse of his mother. If he first could not look at her, he now decides he cannot leave her; however, again he must adjust to life when the attendants routinely drop him at the emergency room before delivering his mother's body. Jack appears never to have managed the situation gracefully; at no time could he maintain himself in the face of death. Finally, he is given a sedative: "And then it came, a miracle of boredom, and he was out" (84). "Out" here suggests that Jack has survived his ordeal; the "miracle of boredom" indicates a numbness that saves. To learn to accept the pressure of death is to go numb, the story seems to say, until time and the hour run through the roughest day.

Such is the idea behind "Flight," which begins in a hunting camp. Dan Ashaway and the narrator have got together every year for hunting, and Dan provides the dogs. But this year death is also in the camp. Ashaway—as his name implies—is ill and is not going to get better. McGuane evokes death with several details. For instance, Ashaway's Dobbs hat and his shotgun are "worn out" (156), and as they ride along, the two hunters watch a hawk kill a sharptail grouse.

Then Ashaway and the narrator participate in the ritual of remembering the old hunting times. These times and the ritual that evokes them give their lives meaning. They are hunters; in hunting they have found their essence and given it to the world. Hunting is their mastered craft, their despair-combating island in a world whose meaning is not clear. They watch the dogs working and take solace in the fluidity of things.

At one point, the narrator begins to panic about Ashaway's impending death—and then must berate himself because he broke the code: one must do what one does well in the face of the final curtain; one must display grace under pressure. After the outburst, which is really no more than a simple question, they listen to the land breathing a sense of itself. Nature again heals. The flow moves on. And with the flow comes death. Ashaway decides, "This is it" (160), and disappears over the hill.

The narrator comments, "Maybe life wasn't something you lost at the end of a long fight. . . . These things can go on and on" (160), a remark that lets us know Ashaway has taken matters into his own hands, shown grace under pressure, and made the ultimate decision not to suffer. He has died according to the hunter's code. In the end, the narrator takes the dogs home. The dogs symbolize the best of Ashaway and the old hunting times; more importantly, however, they represent the ebb and flow of nature, the most powerful law or code, one that hurts but in time and under its own rules also heals.

Unlike so many contemporary short story collections, *To Skin a Cat* provides variety—these stories don't resemble incidents from a novel the author has not had the inspiration to unify. Admittedly, the normal McGuane concerns are evident, yet the stories vary in texture and tone, from his own bleak and almost-sarcastic humor in "Like a Leaf" and "To Skin a Cat" through the satiric view of contemporary values and the pure good-old-boy joy of "A Man in Louisiana" to the settled stoicism of Hemingway in the stories concerned with initiation and death. McGuane's dominating interest is how human beings, whether they are self-absorbed or are concerned for others, confront the discovery of their own vulnerability.

Chapter Ten
Keep the Change:
Drifting toward Meaning

Overview

Thomas McGuane thinks the impetus for *Keep the Change* came from his reading of Chekhov to learn how to write short stories: "There's really nothing to imitate in Chekhov. His work is tantamount to life itself. I remember thinking how important it is to make yourself clear. As you get older, you should get impatient with showing off in literature. It is easier to settle for a blazing light than to find language for the real. Whether you are a writer or a bird dog trainer, life should winnow the superfluous language. The real thing should become plain. You should go straight to what you know best."[1] Concerns that can accurately be labeled "what McGuane knows best" coalesce in *Keep the Change,* the story of Joe Starling, Jr., ersatz son of the soil, artist, illustrator, and the product of his father's lust for success and his own self-absorption with discovering the meaningful life.

Critical Reception

Keep the Change was more widely reviewed than any McGuane book since *Panama,* and it was almost universally praised. Most reviewers like *Newsweek*'s David Gates and the *Atlantic*'s Phoebe-Lou Adams simply find the book to be good reading and praise McGuane for his skillful use of detail.[2] In the *New York Times Book Review,* Beverly Lowry proclaims McGuane "a good writer getting better."[3] She notes perceptively that the early comparison to Hemingway was inaccurate: "From the beginning, [McGuane's] prose had a quality of drop-dead hilarity that put him in a different category." She credits McGuane with caring deeply about his characters and asserts that since *Panama,* McGuane "has expanded his emotional territory and deepened his literary and human concerns" (3).

A Reading

The McGuane set pieces—the impact of the father-son relationship, the quest for a genuine and unique vision, a loving woman who has a mind of her own, a Fitzgeraldian woman who has an agenda of her own, the failure of romanticism in the American West, the crassness of the contemporary consumer society—are all present in *Keep the Change*. But what gives this novel a depth McGuane had heretofore sought but not fully achieved is that author, reader, and protagonist have finally learned that the achievement of wisdom and the discovery of meaning are not the same thing. Joe Starling does not die to make the discovery of his life; nor does he capitulate to middle-class values, escape to a walk-up in Castille, or attempt to fulfill some received notion of the richness of American family life. Joe Starling learns that the acceptance of self-knowledge is as close as he can come to the achievement of wisdom.

Starling is from the very beginning a drifter who fails to take command of his own destiny, and so failing he never develops a sufficiently strong self-concept from which to knowingly face the events of his life. He is victimized by his father's drive for achievement. His father is the "cold blooded Westerner at heart"[4] who realizes that the glorious West does not exist, and abandons his cowboy life for banking. Joe never develops his father's almost-brutal survival instincts. At first, he simply does as he is directed. For instance, he attends military school in Kentucky only because his mother values education. Then he begins to follow his own aimless inclinations. When his parents send him to Yale, he doesn't realize their plan is for Yale to be his first step in building financial security, and so he majors in art.

But the respectable success that results from Joe's career as a painter holds no meaning for him, because he knows that his vision is not really his own. The austere landscapes he paints have their roots in a mysterious painting of the white hills he saw as a child. Once Joe leaves the world of painting, he survives for a time as an illustrator of instruction manuals for useless products. At first content to play a part in the world of creating markets where there is no demand, Joe soon tires of the pointless activity of selling people products they do not need.

Joe does not understand that he is the classic romantic quester, searching for an idealized world he is never going to find. As a youth during a summer in Mexico he falls in love with a prostitute and wastes his money sitting around in a cantina hopelessly dreaming of ways to reform her. He is first attracted to Astrid, a dynamic Cuban who becomes his live-in lover for several years, because she is the most outlandish and spontaneous woman he has ever known. When she turns out to be much more conventional than he supposed, in fact a rather-close-to-normal woman who loves and wants love in return, Joe is at a loss for what to do.

When his life appears to be coming to nothing, Joe makes a frantic run for the abandoned family ranch in Montana in a car stolen from Astrid, only to fall victim to his former sweetheart Ellen Overstreet, the local land baron's daughter. The drama here is classic western. Joe's family ranch is the only land in the region Overstreet does not own, and it makes a painful hole in the map of his dreams; his goal is to achieve a perfect square. At the same time, Joe's less-than-impressive uncle Smitty wants control of the ranch so that he can be an achiever for the first time in his life. Joe's aunt Lureen, in whose name the ranch is actually held, simply wants to live out her retirement in peace, and Joe's presence brings complications she cannot abide. And as with any McGuane protagonist, Joe's major flaw is that he has fallen victim to himself and his idealized notions of the meaning of life: "Everything meant something bigger" (22).

The key to *Keep the Change* is the mysterious painting of the white hills, a painting hanging in an old mansion that came to Joe's father's bank through foreclosure. First seen in flashback, the mansion, which once belonged to the legendary Silver King, is nothing but a ruin. The painting hangs over the fireplace and is barely distinguishable: "It had seemed an unblemished canvas until the perplexity of shadows across its surface was seen to be part of the painting" (2). As the young Joe strains to see something in the picture other than the fearful coldness of life on the upper Missouri River, his father observes that the picture is faded and that there is nothing left. The utterance exactly fits the elder Starling's notion of life in the contemporary West. The real West is nothing like the romanticized popular notion of cowboys living freely on the frontier. Joe, however, protests that the picture is still beautiful, and perhaps surprisingly, his father agrees. We see, then, that both Starlings agree that the West as it lives in the popular imagination is a beautiful thing, even if, as only one of them understands, it cannot be substantiated by real life.

As the novel nears its denouement, the adult Joe Starling, his hopes of generating a new life by returning to the West beginning to crumble around him, returns to the mansion to take a closer look at the painting. In fact, he wants such a close look that he crawls atop the fireplace and stares into the frame at point-blank range. What he discovers is that there is no painting, and that there never has been a painting. The message here is that life in the West is what one makes it, nothing more, nothing less: "Somewhere in the abyss something shone" (215). Joe realizes his father had always grasped this truth; in fact, the elder Starling had claimed this painting was the only one he had ever understood (214). The difficulty Joe Starling encounters while attempting to act on this truth and successfully generate the possibilities of this "something" into meaning is another concern—and the central journey of the novel.

Actual life in the contemporary West is pivotal to the protagonist's quest for meaning. McGuane's earlier notion that the West is a wreck appears to have taken on a deeper complexity here because, unlike *Nobody's Angel*, this novel ultimately portrays the West as not totally disappointing or disillusioning but simply different from the West of both the popular and the protagonist's imaginations.

The new West, however, is certainly not glorious. Joe is no cowboy hero; in fact, he is not comfortable with or confident of his skill at gunplay (221). He finds there is nothing "western" about the old-timers (20); even his father, who certainly can talk the "good old boy talk" turns out to have been a poor rancher because he allowed his place to fall into disrepair even when he was on it full-time (14). There is no longer—and perhaps there never was—reverence for the land itself. Leasing has all but eradicated pride of ownership (62–63). The West is not a land of infinite possibility; rather, it is a place of conservative values where patriotism and conformity are staunchly maintained (16). It is a world where buffalo can be shot and then paid for with a credit card (105), and if anything represents a new frontier, it is that westerners are taking up golf (100). An expert backhoer who can produce perfect foundations and sewer lines becomes the equivalent of the traditional notion of the cowboy becoming one with his horse (80). McGuane makes his point in reverse when he explains that Joe's new horse resembles one in a nineteenth-century photograph by Matthew Brady (83). Brady's idealized notion of the West has become the touchstone against which reality is measured.

Still, for all its lack of romance, this West seems cleaner than the novel's version of American society in general. The larger cultural values seem mired in the nonsense of crass consumerism, presented in the person of Ivan Slater, Joe's college friend and sometime employer. Ivan is a rich businessman with nothing to recommend him except unmitigated gall and a personal religion of optimism in pursuit of money. Ivan develops and markets diverse and outlandish gadgets—such as portable telephones that fasten to clothing, automatic cat feeders, and gas-powered fire logs—and employs Joe to illustrate the instruction manuals that accompany them. Joe sees his audience as "stupid but happy people [trying to understand the] worthless shit" (37) they spend good money on. Meaningful life, we are to understand, can, should, and must be lived free of the pursuit of useless products, which, while perhaps providing leisure, do nothing to enhance the potential of the human spirit.

Ivan will not tolerate Joe's cynical attitude. He sees nothing ridiculous in his products (45), and in fact we understand that the concept of ridiculousness is nonexistent in contemporary American consumer culture. Joe's notion that in giving up painting and going to work for Ivan he has "sold out" (48) seems an anachronism, an allegiance to the values of a forgotten era. There is also an undercurrent of sleaze in Ivan's life. For instance, he proudly announces that his lap-top computer "will do everything but suck you off back at the Ramada" (37). Nothing in Montana approaches such a state of the ridiculous. In the West, land and animals and their attendant problems are at least something real. Like many of McGuane's protagonists, Joe has always managed to find pleasure in the world of the ranch, from fencing (15) through securing loans (78) to moving cattle (86, 169). On his return home Joe invests great hope in the West: as he sees the mountains and the buffalo, his spirits rise (58–59).

McGuane's choice of Starling for his protagonist's family name is auspicious. The starling is a European bird that was not introduced to America until the late 1800s. Like most European immigrants, the starling was introduced in New York and has since spread further into the country. Joe Starling often seems not naturally at home anywhere, especially in Montana, where on his return he is an immigrant in his home country. Although this aspect of dislocation is not new to the McGuane protagonist, Starling's seeming inability to do anything to push himself beyond his own dislocation except to flee in hope of a better world somewhere else makes him distinct in the McGuane canon. In fact, in many ways Joe Starling is refreshingly normal. He is not passionate about competition or violence, he is not motivated by a desire to eschew conformity, he does not withdraw into alcohol, and he does not appear to the outside world to be a victim of self-driven insanity. Essentially, Starling does not know what he wants. Since his formative experiences have given him no strong sense of himself, his life seems to be a matter of response rather than action.

Joe's adolescent involvement with Ellen Overstreet, for instance, appears to result more from the stirrings of the human heart than from any clear notion of macho seduction on Joe's part. Here, too, is another way in which this particular McGuane protagonist is refreshingly new. Joe and Ellen spend long hours simply holding and kissing each other. McGuane is brilliant here as he delineates two adolescents in the halting awakenings of physical lovemaking, the joy inherent in experiencing wet kisses and real breasts. Joe is as interested in "going all the way" as any young person on the threshold of uncovering the possibilities of his or her own body, but he really does not know what to do. Even in his adult sexual relationships with Ellen and Astrid, he is more humanly awkward than any other McGuane protagonist. Until this novel, the McGuane male appears to have been born with the confidence of Casanova.

Unlike previous McGuane protagonists, Starling does not relish rivalry or game playing just for the fun of the conflict or the desire to be the best. His adolescent jealousy over Ellen's concurrent relationship with Billy Kelton, her future husband, stems as much from Joe's grudge against Billy (15) as it does from his being in love with love in his relationship with Ellen. And this grudge is really not of Joe's own making. When Joe and Billy are 13, they get into an argument over a game of horseshoes. Joe's father suggests they "settle this like men" (96). The thought of fighting has not really occurred to either of the boys. Indeed, Billy feels compelled by energy emanating from Joe's father, and Billy is so much stronger than Joe that victory is neither an issue nor a prize. When Billy realizes the pointlessness of harming Joe, Joe's father does not allow him to quit but instead pushes him once more at his son. Both boys are victimized by a set of competitive values they have had no hand in formulating. Joe immediately understands the purposelessness of violence as a way of life, but Billy has to experience Vietnam and several more years of adulthood before he demonstrates that he can act for himself rather than in response to what is expected of him by the macho achievement code so religiously adhered to in American culture, whether by bankers or car mechanics (222).

The scene in which Billy and Joe have their final "showdown" illustrates a new sensitivity in the McGuane canon. There is none of the fun or frolicking of the early novels. Neither we nor the characters are amused; nothing is concocted for laughs. The showdown is set up by a series of misunderstandings. On the surface it looks as if Joe is kidnapping Ellen, and Billy and the town give chase—just like in an old-time western movie. But once the dust settles and everyone expects a final "shoot-out" in which the villain Joe learns his lesson once and for all, Billy simply dismisses the crowd. He and Joe then drive off in Joe's truck. Once into the truck, they talk as two grown men, men whose lives, by their own reckoning, are frustrating and bewildering and—on any scale—not amounting to much. Joe does not feel his ranch is his, because his father's presence there is too strong (224). Billy feels like a failure, for although he is married to the daughter of the most powerful rancher in the territory, he owns nothing. We see a new degree of empathy between rivals here, one that grows from the realization that because life is not theater, it is not something one can simply die and be rid of; rather—and as sentimental as it sounds—life is real and lonely and must be faced not with manic craziness but with middling expectations each and every day. In the face of such truth, there is no room for comic violence.

This inability to live as if one is conquering all of life's adversities differentiates Joe from his father. Joe Starling, Sr., is a new wrinkle on the McGuane father figure. The man is not a comic outlaw, or a well-meaning processor of tasteless foods, or a larger-than-life achiever who dies boldly; he is a man who takes the American success story too seriously, and in the march required to secure his own success and survival, alienates himself from his son, his neighbors, and humanity in general. In the early pages of the novel we see the elder Starling through the eyes of a dutiful son. We understand that he is the only member of his family who became a landholder, and that his real cowboy self is still alive and well beneath his banker's exterior. We sense young Joe's admiration for his father when the text explains that the elder's ambitious quirks, including that of not listening closely to what his son has to say, only make Joe love him more (12). The elder Starling is clearly a man of the West who has understood and confronted the unkind nature of the business world to the point where he is a survivor.

But as the novel unfolds we see he is a victimizer who falls victim to himself. The old-timers knew him as "Sonny," an affectionate moniker suggesting that he was an able learner who earned respect from his cowboy teachers. Once he becomes an officer in the bank, however, Sonny Starling is forced to foreclose on the lands of his friends. He does so without a backward glance. When one such old-timer asserts that the bank made Joe's father "an entirely different feller" and Joe explains that his father is now dead, the oldster replies, "Good" (154). We sense, then, that people and friendships have never meant much to the elder Starling. His need to achieve and his belief in individual survival have driven him beyond a sense of who his real friends—his true people—are.

The elder Starling's life begins to unravel just at the point when by all appearances he should begin to feel he is achieving at a high level; that is, when he is transferred to the corporate headquarters in Minnesota. The text explains that although Minneapolis did not make the Starlings any more happy, they did feel "closer to their view of things" (3). But we must remember that eastern movement in literature is never good for westerners; one moves west toward possibility. For a man like Joe Starling, Sr., a man who lives on expansive achievement, eastward movement is against his natural grain. This factor is apparent in Minnesota when he takes up golf. He plays the sport alone, advancing through slower foursomes at a forced march and accumulating strokes because of impatient putting. Here, then, is the flaw in the elder Starling's character: he has no finesse. Putting, as well as son rearing, requires a gentle touch and the ability to respond to individual situations—various rubs of the green, as it were. He fails to understand the surroundings. His fellow club members not only do not befriend Sonny Starling but also call him "cowboy" because they find him "not suited to civilized life" (7). He is a bold man who belongs outdoors, and he is trying to live in a world that is run from indoors. And more sadly, his obsession with achievement, which far outdistances that necessary for survival—"If you ain't the lead horse, the scenery never changes" (223)—has caused him to leave a world he understands and friends who understand him. In new scenery, on the golf course in the suburbs of Minneapolis, this cowboy rides alone. He does not know the rules.

Finally, his brand of American individualism lets him down and he dies bankrupt. McGuane's text is subtle but crucial here. Joe Starling, Sr., dies alone in his hearselike Buick in the middle of Northfield, Minnesota—a town famous for its rout of the Jesse James gang in the fall of 1876. Like the elder Starling, the James gang had always been successful. They would rob with the same sort of determination Starling employs when playing golf. In the 10 years before the Northfield raid, the James gang enjoyed practically unbridled achievement. They found in the people of Minnesota, however, a kind of stubborn courage they had never confronted in their outlawry in Missouri. Within days of their attempt to rob the First National Bank of Northfield, all the gang members except Frank and Jesse were either killed or captured. The seriously wounded James brothers were hobbling through cornfields in fear of their lives. It was three years before they committed another robbery, and they never again ventured north.[5] The comparison here is not an exact parallel, of course, but what is suggested is that in Minnesota, Jesse James and the elder Starling encounter worlds in which the rules exhibit a power they can neither understand nor control. And both come to ruin.

The real tragedy of the senior Starling is measured in his effect on his son. Ultimately, Joe Starling, Jr., regards his father with almost crippling ambivalence. On the one hand, he admires his cowboy skills and his drive, but on the other, he misses the overt presentation of his father's love and the sense of self-worth and purpose such assurance would bring to him. When his mother admits that his father does not particularly like Joe, he is "quite wounded" (33). Joe has never emotionally risen above the fight his father promoted between Billy Kelton and himself. His father claims the incident was necessary so that Joe would see the damage his best friend could do him and would thus learn not to trust anyone (96). This cliché from the mythology of self-reliance backfires, however, because the incident remains forever terrible to Joe, who is simply made of gentler stuff.

The extent of the damage done when father and son fail to achieve mutual understanding can be seen in the dream Joe has after the first fight with Billy. In his dream Joe joins a band of Indians who attack a white settlement. A couple strongly resembling Joe's parents come out to plead with the war party, but the Indians will not stop, and systematically reduce the settlement to the original prairie grasses (97). The dream seems to suggest two points: (a) that if Joe's father's way is the white way—the American way—then better to give the country back to the Indians, and (b) that brute and merciless force, Indian or white, can serve no positive purpose; nothing productive can come from one opponent obliterating another. That Joe feels somewhat obliterated in his relationship with his father is apparent near the end of the novel, when Joe dreams that the spirit of his father visits in the middle of the night. Joe begins to believe that the motivation for his return to Montana is to take back his name (208). When he thinks of taking back his name here, we understand that he means to establish his own identity, to free himself from the oppressive identity of his father. He is, after all, a "junior" and in the very act of naming, "juniors" inherit legacies that may or may not be compatible with their natures. Were he to establish control over his own name, Joe Starling might have a stronger sense of his own identity, and ultimately, of his own purpose and meaning independent in themselves and not in relation to those of his father.

That he has no distinct sense of himself is clear in Joe's relationships with the major female characters in *Keep the Change*. Ellen and Astrid are McGuane's most fully realized and complex females. Ellen Overstreet is McGuane's Fitzgeraldian woman, the one who ultimately abuses the protagonist because all along she has been adhering to her own goal. But Ellen has more depth than her earlier incarnations. Unlike Ann in *Bushwhacked Piano*, Ellen is not presented for satire; neither is she as completely hard and selfish as Claire Burnett appears in *Nobody's Angel*. Nor is Ellen a hip, wisecracking creation of male fantasy. When we first see her she is a teenager encountering Joe during the summer before he graduates from the military academy. They both try at first to act out of a sophistication neither possesses. When their verbal sparing tones down to school subjects and a series of "O wow's" (17), we understand that she is a sweet, unassuming country teenager.

More importantly, Ellen and Joe have a real friendship, involving ranch work, horseback riding, and discovery of the backcountry. It is clear from the beginning that these simple pleasures are and will always be the full extent of Ellen's world. For instance, she does not know the peace sign (18) or recognize the name Rockefeller (99). She thinks one of Joe's paintings looks like custard next to a house (99). She understands neither his work nor his frantic need for meaning. Her most endearing quality is simple honesty. When Joe returns to the ranch to find himself, she immediately tells him that although she will see him, she and her estranged husband, Billy Kelton, are trying to save their marriage (91).

It is true that Ellen lies to Joe when she tells him he is the father of her daughter, Clara. But in this instance she is victimized by her adherence to one of the major tenets of the world she inhabits: unfailing devotion to her men. The lie is her father's idea because he never-endingly desires the Starling ranch. She too is victimized in her relationship with Joe. In his desire to discover purpose, Joe does not really see Ellen for who she is but immediately imbues her with too much meaning. Since she teaches at the grade school he attended (91–92), she embodies the innocence of his past—an innocence he is hoping to recapture. And she provides him with a ready-made daughter, launching him on a fulfilling fantasy of fatherhood. In his mind, Ellen hands him at once a useful past and a potent future.

Ellen's adult sexual relationship with Joe is not cynical; she has not set out to "have been around" or to "commit experience" in the deliberate and manipulating way of earlier McGuane female characters. Early on she innocently jokes that she and Joe will create a scandal simply by eating together (99). That she consumes a 16-ounce rib eye at this dinner indicates more that she is a healthy countrywoman than that she is voracious for "man meat." If anything, her fling with Joe can be seen as simple curiosity. True, her first physical experience was with Joe, but his momentary penetration and adolescent bewilderment (27) hardly qualify as lovemaking. Ellen may interpret the fact that her husband is involved in an affair as justification to experiment, and Joe still represents a person from outside her own world, an opportunity for an adventure that may present itself only once.

Whatever the case, we see eventually that Ellen feels she has been more honest in their relationship than Joe has. During the truck race that leads to the final conversation between Joe and Billy, Joe insinuates that the whole predicament is Ellen's fault and calls her a "stupid bitch [and a] rotten crumb" (220). She responds that they may be having their first-ever serious conversation: "Are you telling me that it is possible I could mean more to you than pussy or golf lessons? . . . I could actually rise in your esteem to the status of 'stupid bitch'? Oh, this *is* romantic" (220). Her feelings here could well be deep-seated, generating from their relationship as teenagers. Joe, after all, is the one who left town, and we can assume that since he did not know whom Ellen married or what she was doing, he is the one who lost interest. Ellen senses that her importance to Joe rests largely in his fictional fatherhood and that their physical couplings have meant little more than biology to him. Anger is at least an honest emotion, and the presence of such honesty in Joe surprises her. Even though Ellen's use of the word *romantic* is tinged with irony, it reinforces her genuine need for essential honesty. Had she and Joe been honest with each other, romance might have been possible. It is, after all, the essential honesty of the love shared by Billy and Clara and herself that draws Ellen back to her family.

When Joe is seeing Ellen, he wishes to rid his mind of Astrid, the dynamic Cuban woman (99). When Joe's first attempt to make love to the adult Ellen fails, he blames the fiasco on Astrid's voodoo (119). Indeed, all through the novel Joe cannot determine whether he loves or hates Astrid. He experiences this dilemma because McGuane has developed a fine character who consumes Joe's consciousness for the simple reason that she knows him too well and will not support his seemingly adolescent search for self. Astrid pursues Joe to Montana and variously tells him he has no conviction (147), mocks him as a "man in translation" (141), and most appropriately calls him a "dimestore Hamlet" (128). Astrid is a reverse image of Catherine in *Panama* and Suzanne in *Something to Be Desired*. Though given to craziness, she is ultimately the one who wants a stable life, and she becomes impatient with Joe's constant search for meaning, his insistence that everything means something more. We understand that the trouble with Astrid is that she is not the woman Joe thought he was falling in love with.

Joe is first attracted to Astrid for her outlandishness. For instance, the first time he sees her she is painted gold, going to a party as a hood ornament (35). At one point she spontaneously fells him with fellatio while he is trying to read his mail (43). At another point she makes the wonderfully bizarre remark "I wish I was back in Florida, fucking and using drugs" (145). Joe, committed to the notion that everything has to mean something more, aggrandizes everything she does. He defines her penchant for neatness as "city ways" (131), is fascinated when her shower-wet hair soaks the shoulders of her dress (140), and sees her as helpless and dependent when she is merely ill (144). Of course what she is, is sick of Montana. She knows Joe's only hope for survival lies in the one thing he continually refuses to do: return to his painting. She does not care whether Joe feels his work is authentic or not. The problem is that Astrid is only outlandish on the surface; underneath she is too real for Joe. She wants domesticity, conventional fun in the sun, that old-fashioned thing called a love relationship.

The tensions in both relationships are the same. Ellen and Astrid derive meaning from the knowledge that they mean something to someone else. Joe simply seems unable to accept the notion that the profound meaning he seeks may well lie in devotion to the ordinary commitments of life. After all, his best days with Astrid "turned upon ordinariness" (168). When all have performed their tragic play, the text seems to say, the true meaning of life lies in the strength of one's relationships, in the durability of the bonding. That this point would be unclear to Joe is apparent from a look at his own family. He stems from "unassuming people mad with greed and desire for fame or love" (9–10). His grandmother thought her own sons were swindlers (162), and his grandfather was an angry man whose discipline bordered on child abuse and who was blind in one eye (178). The single vision here is symbolic of those who are out for themselves, of the monomaniacal quest of Sonny Starling. Joe is like his father, although he is not as violent and insensitive. He is self-absorbed in his desire to discover his meaning and sense of self—the "something" in the mysterious painting of the white hills.

Some key details from the novel indicate the nature of Joe's search. His banker tells him he is too nineteenth-century in his hopes for the ranch (79). The difference between the preceding century and this one is that the West is now without the very element Joe Starling requires: infinite possibility. He thinks he is not required to learn to live in any of his various worlds, because his mind is locked into the idea that life has no limits. For instance, he senses true freedom in movement (51, 208). He demonstrates important self-knowledge when he admits he is not the type to stay and work through problems (225). That he is at heart a nomad is reinforced when he senses kinship with an ancient Indian through the touch of an arrowhead (191). We understand as well that his search is an individual one. He does not trust duos (182). When he speaks of *his* love for Astrid, it is *his* feelings toward her that really matter to him. It was his father who taught him about life's unbearable loneliness, not only during the fight with Billy Kelton but once when Joe was trying to make his father see that he was an alcoholic. He recorded his father drunk and played the tape the next morning (184). The result—like most of Joe's adventures—was not what he had hoped. Showing another person the truth about him- or herself is not a kind act. Even though Joe had wanted the disclosure to bring him closer to his father, they became permanently estranged—Joe is alone even though there is another human being in the world with the same name as his. He is, through predilection and circumstance, a natural isolato.

This tendency toward individualism frustrates Joe's acceptance of his painting career as his true destiny. He knows his style and viewpoint are based on an "undiscovered plagiary" (2); despite his success, he has contributed nothing unique, nothing self-generated. His career, then, at bottom means nothing to him (31). This factor is what drives him back to Montana to discover the "something" in the painting of the white hills. Yet the only real discovery Joe makes is that "everything takes place in time" (223), a discovery that breaks his heart because he knows nothing lasts forever, and more seriously, because the events of his life do not build step by step toward some great whole. He has told his various worlds to "keep the change"—moving on without waiting for what might come to him were he to stay and conquer his disappointments and attempt to build a foundation—and sadly, he has moved on without changing. In the end, Joe has simply lived many lives. His hope for the West is ultimately empty because the West he is looking for does not exist, and—if symbolic overtones can be attributed to Ellen and Billy's feebleminded child as an heir to the West and symbol of Joe's imagined future—the West manifesting such possibility as Joe seeks will never come into being.

There are hints that Joe might someday realize that true significance can be found in ordinariness and in relationships. His two great gifts of self are when he restores a maggot-ridden dog (90) and when he gives his ranch to Billy Kelton out of compassion and respect (225). That Astrid takes the dog with her when she leaves is important, for the dog is a manifestation of a non-self-absorbed Joe. And as the novel ends, Joe is thinking again of trying to re-form his relationship with Astrid; she is the one element in his life that is not frozen in time. It is Astrid, after all, who has told Joe the most important thing he needs to learn, understand, and know: "You can't have what you want every minute of the day" (140). As Joe sits beneath the Crazy Mountains wet with early snow—the actual beautiful white hills—preparing to take up his search again, Astrid remains the most dynamic force in his life, the real springboard to hope.

Chapter Eleven
The Future of a Person of Letters

As he ponders his future, Thomas McGuane maintains a farsighted view of the art that has consumed the enthusiasm of a lifetime:

It would be well for writers not to think about their importance. I've been . . . writing for 30 years, and what it amounts to is, you either do good work or you don't. The future will be a fair judge of my worth. I think I am getting more control of the craft. Writer and protagonist are always on the verge of wisdom. They struggle to find it, but don't always. It's a terrible struggle to find language. I have to keep doing this. You can't keep trading cars till you get a perfect one. You have to just decide to stick it out. Faulkner is unreadable a lot of the time. But where he is not unreadable he is completely worth all the time you've put in. If you are going to accept that particular writer for that particular hour, you have to accept that that writer is trying to reveal things.

While it may be too early in McGuane's career to comfortably accord him an uncontested seat in the American canon, we have no difficulty acknowledging that his revelations are in the center of the American grain. His so-far-always-male protagonists seem generated from the myth of the frontier, American Adams who demand worlds of infinite possibility and who will in fact consider achieving actualization in no other. McGuane's fictions are, however, decidedly twentieth-century, in that protagonists who quest for frontier worlds are perpetually alienated from the mainstream of contemporary life. They are metaphorical orphans, often existing without nurture from family ties. Such solitary and expansive sensibilities seemingly have no place to flourish. A look at McGuane's oeuvre, however, reveals that his continually developing protagonists are not defeated simply because they are dislocated, and in their more mature guises, they work to accommodate infinite hopes within the strictures of contemporary reality without any loss of self.

They become twentieth-century versions of the isolato, sometimes equipped with practical notions and great respect for craft, for professionalism, and for business that fulfills rather than denigrates. Like frontiersmen in the new Eden, McGuane protagonists come into full being in nature, very often working the land or horses. At the same time, they register a great longing for the romanticized, transcendent possibilities of the nineteenth century—the mythologies embodied in Pecos Bill and Jesse James—that free their imaginations from daily and mundane concerns. They seek to "have it both ways," to live lives that realize myth and reality at the same time. For the most part, they do not accept defeat in quest of this seemingly impossible goal but instead maintain a truly Emersonian sense of optimism. Only momentarily do McGuane's recent protagonists take refuge in manic craziness. Vernor Stanton and Nicholas Payne have grown older. Seemingly coming to fruition from a seed planted in the character of James Quinn, later protagonists Lucien Taylor and Joe Starling no longer seek to remain "at large" in the transcendent sense. Although these two meet with varying degrees of success, they seem more concerned with shaping a life in America than with imprinting their consciousnesses on the nation itself. No longer like Patrick Fitzpatrick or Chester Pomeroy, McGuane protagonists seem to want to build something lasting, announcing in their way that life is no longer cheap, no longer easily wasted on discord.

Like the sensibilities of the American canon's foremost writers, McGuane's emerging sensibility both mirrors and instructs. Life seems to have taught both him and his protagonists. Violence seems no longer inherently comic, despair inherently amusing. His female characters are no longer supporting players unable to match wits with his male ones. Movement toward fulfillment—that phenomenon so crucial to frontier exploration—seems possible on a smaller, more inwardly liberating scale. That McGuane's protagonists have gone through rage, rebellion, and defeat before discovering rebirth has yielded a stronger sense of self, one that need not be continually testing itself against the absurdity that surrounds them. Both protagonist and writer seek to create order out of the chaos of contemporary life. They develop both a self-knowledge and a universal awareness that inspire continued hope that as we near the beginning of the twenty-first century, we can combine the energies of the self-creating and the practical to eradicate the disparities between our sense of the ideal—an America with a unique sense of its own worth and destiny—and the crass commercialism and homogenizing reality that constitute daily experience in our time.

Notes and References

Preface

1. For an understanding of the contributions of Seymour Lawrence and Gary Fisketjon to contemporary serious fiction, see Robert A. Carter, "Seymour Lawrence," *Publishers Weekly*, 17 March 1989, 20–22, and E. Graydon Carter, "Leading the Gliterary Life," *Esquire*, December 1986, 161–66.

Chapter One

1. Interview with author, 25–26 July 1988, McLeod, Montana. Unless otherwise noted, all statements attributed to Thomas McGuane are from this interview.
2. "The Art of Fiction 89," interview with Sinda Gregory and Larry McCaffery, *Paris Review* (Fall 1985):50.
3. "Thomas McGuane: An Interview," interview with Albert Howard Carter III, *Fiction International* 4–5 (1975):55.
4. "The Art of Fiction," 45.
5. *An Outside Chance: Essays on Sport* (New York: Farrar, Straus & Giroux, 1980), 159–60.
6. Ibid., 97.
7. Ibid., 98.
8. "The Art of Fiction," 51.
9. Ibid., 47.
10. Ibid., 48.
11. "The Novelist in Hollywood: An Interview with Thomas McGuane," interview with Leonard Michaels, *Threepenny Review* 1 (Winter 1981):5.
12. "Thomas McGuane: An Interview," 54.
13. "A Conversation with Thomas McGuane," interview with Liz Lear, *Shenandoah* 36 (1986):13.
14. James Atlas, "Writing the Range," *Vanity Fair,* April 1986, 96.
15. Jim Harrison, telephone interview with author, 20 October 1988. All statements attributed to Jim Harrison are from this interview.
16. Thomas Carney, "McGuane's Game," *Esquire,* 6 June 1978, 45.
17. William Hjortsberg, telephone interview with author, 13 December 1988. All statements attributed to William Hjortsberg are from this interview.
18. Michael Palmer, telephone interview with author, 18 December 1988. All statements attributed to Michael Palmer are from this interview.
19. "An Interview with Tom McGuane," interview with Kay Bonetti, *Missouri Review* 9 (1985–86):79.

20. "The Art of Fiction," 37.

21. "An Interview with Tom McGuane," 79.

22. John Dorschner, "Portrait of the Author as a Young Director," *Miami Herald,* 13 October 1974, reprinted in *Authors in the News,* vol. 2 (Detroit: Gale Research, 1976), 196.

23. "A Conversation with Thomas McGuane," 13.

24. Carney, "McGuane's Game," 44.

25. Lawrence Wright, "The Life and Death of Richard Brautigan," *Rolling Stone,* 11 April 1985, 38.

26. Carney, "McGuane's Game," 45.

27. Ibid.

28. Dorschner, "Portrait of the Author as a Young Director," 194.

29. Ibid.

30. Michael Tolkin, "*92 in the Shade,* 86'd in the Smog," *Village Voice,* 15 September 1975, 124.

31. Ibid.

32. Ibid., 125.

33. "The Art of Fiction," 69.

34. Gregory Skwira, "From Best Seller to Burnout and Back," *Chicago Tribune,* 12 April 1985, sec. 5, p. 3.

35. "The Novelist in Hollywood," 5.

36. Judson Klinger, "In Pursuit of Crazy Language," *American Film,* April 1989, 64.

37. Ibid., 60.

38. "An Interview with Tom McGuane," 95.

39. Atlas, "Writing the Range," 117.

40. "The Art of Fiction," 49.

41. "An Interview with Tom McGuane," 77.

42. Ibid., 87.

43. Ibid., 83.

44. *An Outside Chance,* 213.

45. "The Art of Fiction," 71.

46. *An Outside Chance,* 222.

47. "The Art of Fiction," 52.

48. Ibid., 70.

49. "A Conversation with Thomas McGuane," 19.

50. Russell Martin, "Writers of the Purple Sage," *New York Times Magazine,* 27 December 1981, 18.

51. "An Interview with Tom McGuane," 88.

52. "The Art of Fiction," 56–57.

53. "An Interview with Tom McGuane," 90.

54. "The Art of Fiction," 62.

55. Ibid., 47.

56. "An Interview with Tom McGuane," 99.

57. Ibid., 82.

Chapter Two

1. Joyce Carol Oates, review of *The Sporting Club, New York Times Book Review*, 23 March 1969, 5. Subsequent citation is noted in the text.

2. John Leonard, "Lethal Games Some People Play," review of *The Sporting Club, Life*, 7 March 1969, 8.

3. Sara Blackburn, review of *The Sporting Club, Nation*, 14 April 1969, 475.

4. Linda Kuehl, review of *The Sporting Club, Commonweal*, 26 December 1969, 385.

5. Review of *The Sporting Club, Times Literary Supplement*, 21 August 1969, 927.

6. *An Outside Chance*, 175.

7. *The Sporting Club* (New York: Penguin Books, 1979), 24. All subsequent citations are to this edition.

Chapter Three

1. *The Bushwhacked Piano* (New York: Vintage Books, 1984), 34. All subsequent citations are to this edition.

2. J. D. O'Hara, review of *The Bushwhacked Piano, Saturday Review*, 27 March 1971, 48. Subsequent citation is noted in the text.

3. L. E. Sissman, "Inventions," review of *The Bushwhacked Piano, New Yorker*, 11 September 1971, 124. Subsequent citation is noted in the text.

4. Jonathan Yardley, review of *The Bushwhacked Piano, New York Times Book Review*, 14 March 1971, 6. Subsequent citation is noted in the text.

Chapter Four

1. *Ninety-two in the Shade* (New York: Penguin Books, 1980), 174. All subsequent citations are to this edition.

2. An interesting sidelight here is that in an early incarnation of the film version (*92 in the Shade*, with Peter Fonda, Warren Oates, Margot Kidder, Elizabeth Ashley, Burgess Meredith, Sylvia Miles, and Harry Dean Stanton; United Artists, 1975) written and directed by McGuane, Skelton does not make the discovery of his life, because he does not die. Instead, Skelton and Dance sit in Skelton's boat, warmly pounding each other's back in true macho friendship. In his 1975 interview with Albert Howard Carter, McGuane claims the ending is not a Hollywood cop-out, because it is all right for the two adversaries to violate their principles given their mutual affection. In his 1985 interview with Sinda Gregory and Larry McCaffery, however, McGuane explains that he shot two endings, one with Skelton alive and one with him dead. He allows that the one that is faithful to

the book is the better ending. The available VHS cassette version (Key Video, 1986) ends as Dance shoots Skelton.

3. Walter Clemons, "Collision in the Keys," review of *Ninety-two in the Shade, Newsweek*, 23 July 1973, 71.

4. Thomas R. Edwards, review of *Ninety-two in the Shade, New York Times Book Review*, 29 July 1973, 2. Subsequent citation is noted in the text.

5. Martha Duffy, "Papa's Son," review of *Ninety-two in the Shade, Time*, 6 August 1973, 70.

6. L. E. Sissman, "Living by the Sword," review of *Ninety-two in the Shade, New Yorker*, 23 June 1973, 87. Subsequent citation is noted in the text.

7. Richard Todd, review of *Ninety-two in the Shade, Atlantic Monthly*, September 1973, 105.

Chapter Five

1. Frank Perry, dir., *Rancho DeLuxe*, with Jeff Bridges, Sam Waterston, Elizabeth Ashley, Charlene Dallas, Clifton James, Slim Pickens, and Harry Dean Stanton; United Artists, 1975.

2. Frontier rifles take on a symbolic impact of their own in the McGuane screenplays. Appearing in 1848, the Sharps rifle, a big-bore breechloader, became immediately the standard weapon for killing buffalo. Its accuracy could be counted on for 200 yards, and it could function with either cartridges or powder and ball. (Larry Koller, *The Fireside Book of Guns* [New York: Simon & Schuster, 1959], 93–94.) In owning the Sharps, Jack and Cecil link themselves with the fabled buffalo hunters of the plains.

The Creedmore carried by Lee Clayton in *The Missouri Breaks* was a special target model version of the Sharps buffalo gun. It was a .44-caliber breechloader that could successfully hit targets up to 1,000 yards away. Thus, Tom Logan can define "regulator" as someone who kills people and "don't ever come near em." The Creedmore became popular as a result of its use in the First International Rifle Match at Creedmore, Long Island, in 1874. American shooters used Creedmores to barely turn back the Irish Wimbledon champions (60–61). In the film Marlon Brando appears to be indulging in a bit of irony when he characterizes Lee Clayton talking continually in an Irish accent.

McGuane's private irony appears to be present in *Tom Horn* because the Winchester 45/60 carried by Horn was manufactured in 1876 and called the Centennial (169–70), no doubt in honor of the first 100 years of a nation founded on the notion of individual freedom. In the early years of the twentieth century Horn's brand of freedom is no longer possible. Indeed, he spends the final section of the screenplay in jail, staring at the hills he is no longer free to roam.

Of interest here is that in the first three screenplays, the rifles, so necessary to the myth of the lone frontiersman, lead to the downfalls of those who live by them. Horn and Clayton, men no longer at one with their times, perish. Only in the contemporary West are the would-be plainsmen Jack and Cecil afforded the ironical twist of surviving their downfall: the Sharps rifle leads to their capture, and once captured, they are "free" (that is, not hindered by the conventions of the twentieth century) to be real cowboys on Rancho DeLuxe.

3. *Nobody's Angel* (New York: Random House, 1981), 123. All subsequent citations are to this edition.

4. Arthur Penn, dir., *Missouri Breaks*, with Marlon Brando, Jack Nicholson, Randy Quaid, Kathleen Lloyd, Frederick Forrest, and Harry Dean Stanton; United Artists, 1976.

5. Letter to author, 14 March 1985.

6. *The Missouri Breaks* (New York: Ballantine, 1976), 122. All subsequent citations are to this edition.

7. William Wiard, dir., *Tom Horn,* with Steve McQueen, Linda Evans, Richard Farnsworth, Billy Green Bush, and Slim Pickens; Warner Brothers, 1980.

8. Bud Shrake, telephone interview with author, 27 October 1984. All statements attributed to Bud Shrake are from this interview.

9. Letter to author, 31 October 1984.

10. Robert Dornhelm, dir., *Cold Feet*, with Keith Carradine, Sally Kirkland, Tom Waits, Bill Pullman, Rip Torn, and Kathleen York; Avenue Pictures, 1989. My comments on *Cold Feet* are based on a reading of the shooting script.

Chapter Six

1. "The Art of Fiction," 43.

2. *Panama* (New York: Farrar, Straus & Giroux, 1978), 154. All subsequent citations are to this edition.

3. Review of *Panama, Time,* 13 November 1978, 123.

4. Richard Elman, review of *Panama, New York Times Book Review,* 19 November 1978, 36.

5. Donald R. Katz, "Thomas McGuane: Heroes in 'Hotcakesland,'" *New Republic*, 18 August 1979, 38. Subsequent citation is noted in the text.

6. Gary Fisketjon, review of *Panama, Village Voice,* 11 December 1978, 115.

7. Susan Lardner, "McGuane Again," review of *Panama, New Yorker,* 9 April 1979, 156. Subsequent citation is noted in the text.

8. See also Kerry Grant, "On and Off the Main Line: The Failure of Compromise in the Fiction of Thomas McGuane," *Mid-American Review* 3 (Spring 1983), 174–75.

Chapter Seven

1. Jeffrey Brodrick, "A New Gig," review of *Nobody's Angel, National Review,* 11 June 1982, 704.

2. Review of *Nobody's Angel, New Yorker,* 22 March 1982, 165.

3. Ken Tucker, review of *Nobody's Angel, Village Voice*, 20 April 1982, 41.

4. Richard Stengel, "Hurtin' Cowboy," review of *Nobody's Angel, Time*, 26 April 1982, 18.

5. Ray Sawhill, "Burnt-out Case," review of *Nobody's Angel, Newsweek*, 29 March 1982, 73–74.

6. Geoffrey Stokes, "Hung Over in Montana," review of *Nobody's Angel, Nation*, 20 March 1982, 341. Subsequent citation is noted in the text.

7. Vance Bourjaily, "The Story of a Superfluous Man," review of *Nobody's Angel, New York Times Book Review*, 7 March 1982, 9. Subsequent citation is noted in the text.

8. See also Jon Wallace, "Speaking against the Dark: Style as Theme in Thomas McGuane's *Nobody's Angel*," *Modern Fiction Studies* 33 (Summer 1987), 292–96.

9. See also Charles G. Masinton, "*Nobody's Angel:* Thomas McGuane's Vision of the Contemporary West, *New Mexico Humanities Review* 6 (Fall 1983), 52–53.

Chapter Eight

1. Walter Clemons, review of *Something to Be Desired, Newsweek*, 21 January 1985, 71.

2. Robert Roper, "Lucien Alone in Deadrock," review of *Something to Be Desired, New York Times Book Review*, 16 December 1984, 11. Subsequent citation is in the text.

3. *Something to Be Desired* (New York: Random House, 1984), 145. All subsequent citations are to this edition.

4. Interview on National Public Radio by Noah Adams, 25 October 1984.

5. Ibid.

Chapter Nine

1. Elizabeth Tallent, "The Sign of Life Is Mayhem," review of *To Skin a Cat, New York Times Book Review*, 19 October 1986, 13. Subsequent citation is in the text.

2. *To Skin a Cat* (New York: E. P. Dutton/Seymour Lawrence, 1986), 40. All subsequent citations are to this edition.

3. "To Skin a Cat," *TriQuarterly* 50 (Winter 1981), 36. Subsequent citation is in the text.

Chapter Ten

1. Telephone interview with author, 6 August 1989.

2. David Gates, review of *Keep the Change, Newsweek*, 18 September 1989, 76; Phoebe-Lou Adams, review of *Keep the Change, Atlantic*, October 1989, 115.

3. Beverly Lowry, "A Manly Man Takes His Act on the Road," review of

Keep the Change, New York Times Book Review, 24 September 1989, 3. Subsequent citation is in the text.

4. *Keep the Change* (Boston: Houghton Mifflin/Seymour Lawrence, 1989), 5. All subsequent citations are to this edition.

5. Paul I. Wellman, *A Dynasty of Western Outlaws* (Lincoln: University of Nebraska Press, 1986), 95–110.

Selected Bibliography

PRIMARY WORKS

The Bushwhacked Piano. New York: Simon & Schuster, 1971; New York: Vintage Books, 1984.

Keep the Change. Boston: Houghton Mifflin/Seymour Lawrence, 1989; New York: Vintage Books, 1990.

The Missouri Breaks. New York: Ballantine, 1976.

Ninety-two in the Shade. New York: Farrar, Straus & Giroux, 1973; New York: Penguin Books, 1979.

Nobody's Angel. New York: Random House, 1982; New York: Vintage Books, 1986.

An Outside Chance: Essays on Sport. New York: Farrar, Straus & Giroux, 1980; New York: Penguin Books, 1982.

Panama. New York: Farrar, Straus & Giroux, 1978; New York: Penguin Books, 1980.

Something to Be Desired. New York: Random House, 1984; New York: Vintage Books, 1985.

The Sporting Club. New York: Simon & Schuster, 1969; New York: Penguin Books, 1979.

To Skin a Cat. New York: E. P. Dutton/Seymour Lawrence, 1986; New York: Vintage Books, 1987.

SECONDARY WORKS

Carter, Albert Howard, III. "Thomas McGuane's First Three Novels: Games, Fun, Nemesis." *Critique* 17 (August 1975): 91–104. Games point up the interaction between pathos and humor. A good introduction to McGuane and his ideas at an early stage of his career.

Grant, Kerry. "On and Off the Main Line: The Failure of Compromise in the Fiction of Thomas McGuane." *Mid-American Review* 3 (Spring 1983): 167–84. McGuane protagonists understand that they must compromise with reality, but they cannot resist the urge to imprint their unique selves on the boundaries of life. Very good.

Klinkowitz, Jerome. *The New American Novel of Manners: The Fiction of Richard Yates, Dan Wakefield, and Thomas McGuane.* Athens: University of

Georgia Press, 1986. Since social conventions are signs in our linguistic system, these three novelists are semioticians of the postmodernist age.

Masinton, Charles G. "*Nobody's Angel:* Thomas McGuane's Vision of the Contemporary West." *New Mexico Humanities Review,* 6 (Fall 1983): 49–55. McGuane's sense of the wrecked West, which runs from absurdity to pessimism, can be seen in *Rancho DeLuxe* and *Nobody's Angel.* Insightful analysis.

McCaffery, Larry. "On Turning Nothing into Something." *Fiction International* 4–5 (Fall–Winter 1975): 123–29. McGuane mirrors and criticizes American culture, but at the same time the final effect of his work is transcendence, because his protagonists seek to maintain their ideals despite existential despair. Another good introduction to the early McGuane.

Wallace, Jon. "The Language Plot in Thomas McGuane's *Ninety-two in the Shade.*" *Critique* 29 (Winter 1988): 111–20. To make sense of life and self, the narrator mixes language codes as a way of arguing against the depersonalizing effects of American culture. Insightful.

————. "Speaking against the Dark: Style as Theme in Thomas McGuane's *Nobody's Angel.*" *Modern Fiction Studies* 33 (Summer 1987): 289–98. The narrator is a character in a fragmented world, seeking to find himself through style. Asserts that language is McGuane's main concern.

Welch, Dennis M. "Death and Fun in the Novels of Thomas McGuane." *Windsor Review* 14 (Fall/Winter 1978): 14–20. McGuane's protagonists do not negate mortality; rather, they choose to confront it with a playful attitude and in the process keep themselves open to the possibilities of life. Useful work with the first three novels.

Index

The Author

Dexter Westrum received his B.A. from Sioux Falls College and his M.A. and Ph.D. from the University of Minnesota. Since 1985 he has taught British and American literature at Ottawa University in Kansas. The student body awarded him O.U. Oscars in 1987 for Best Overall Faculty Member and in 1988 for Most Supporting Faculty Member; the class of 1988 named him Most Distinguished Professor. His short stories, book reviews, and critical essays have appeared in numerous professional journals, little magazines, and anthologies in this country and in Canada.

The Editor

Frank Day is a professor of English at Clemson University. He is the author of *Sir William Empson: An Annotated Bibliography* and *Arthur Koestler: A Guide to Research*. He was a Fulbright lecturer in American literature in Romania (1980–81) and in Bangladesh (1986–87).